The Stone Soup Experiment

The Stone Soup Experiment

Why Cultural Boundaries Persist

Deborah Downing Wilson

The University of Chicago Press

Chicago and London

Deborah Downing Wilson is an instructor in the Department of Communication at the University of Nevada, Reno.

The University of Chicago Press, Chicago 60637
The University of Chicago Press, Ltd., London
© 2015 by The University of Chicago
All rights reserved. Published 2015.
Printed in the United States of America

24 23 22 21 20 19 18 17 16 15 1 2 3 4 5

ISBN-13: 978-0-226-28977-9 (cloth)
ISBN-13: 978-0-226-28980-9 (paper)
ISBN-13: 978-0-226-28994-6 (e-book)
DOI: 10.7208/chicago/9780226289946.001.0001

Library of Congress Cataloging-in-Publication Data
Wilson, Deborah Downing, author.
    The stone soup experiment : why cultural boundaries persist / Deborah
Downing Wilson.
        pages ; cm
    Includes bibliographical references and index.
    ISBN 978-0-226-28977-9 (cloth : alk. paper) — ISBN 978-0-226-28980-9
(pbk : alk. paper) — ISBN 978-0-226-28994-6 (ebook) 1. Cultural relations—
Cross-cultural studies. 2. Intergroup relations—Cross-cultural studies. 3. Group
identity—Cross-cultural studies. 4. Social interaction—Cross-cultural studies.
5. Social psychology—Methodology. 6. Psychology, Experimental. I. Title.
    HM623.W55 2015
    303.48′2—dc23

                                                                    2015007464

♾ This paper meets the requirements of ANSI/NISO Z39.48–1992 (Permanence of
Paper).

For Bernice and Harry

CONTENTS

The Romantic Classroom

Insofar as we make use of our healthy senses, we ourselves are the
best and most exact scientific instruments possible.

Goethe, *Verses in Prose*[1]

In spring 2008 my students and I entered into a cultural simulation game
as part of a participatory science investigation. The game was designed to
expose the processes through which culture emerges in newly forming
groups and to reveal the ways in-group members develop common understandings among themselves. As a researcher I hoped to see evidence of the
students' identification with their groups, the invention and elaboration
of cultural conventions and materials, as well as the borrowing and adaptation of cultural products from other groups when they came in contact
with each other. Despite some hints from the relevant literature, the strong
emotional investments demonstrated by all participants surprised me, as
did the almost immediate formation of well-defined in-group versus out-
group boundaries, the complexity and intensity of the negotiations that
took place when these boundaries were breached, and the sustained identification with the "natal" groups long after the simulation phase of the investigation was over. I was completely unprepared for the stealing, cheating,
lying, conspiracy, and betrayal that sent the project careening in entirely
unexpected ways. And I certainly did not expect to be consumed by the

group competition in a way that distorted my perspective and made impartial analyses impossible.

I have three interrelated goals in writing this book. First, I offer an insider's account of the genesis of culture in small groups, conceptualized here as a collective narrative process—that is, a creative meaning-making endeavor that entails ongoing negotiation and compromise as well as the synchronization of new and previously learned systems of symbols and practices.

Second, I chronicle the implementation of a pedagogical model and research strategy known as romantic science. As part 1 describes in more detail, romantic science emphasizes the lived experiences of the participating observers and incorporates the researchers' "scientific knowing" with their feelings as they explore new areas of knowledge in relationship with others. These feelings are understood here not as secondary or auxiliary forms of understanding, but as key elements of our cognitive and communication processes.

Finally, I share my new appreciation for social simulations as powerful tools for both teaching and research in the social sciences. Not only did the simulation quickly and efficiently bring forty-four people together in meaningful relationships, but it evoked a measure of affective investment rarely experienced in college classrooms. Once engaged in the simulation, what began as a game became real, enabling participants to draw conclusions that applied to their everyday life experiences outside of the simulation. The students' narratives, included throughout the text, clearly reveal this blurred distinction between play and "real life." This blurring, I believe, has valuable implications for those seeking to understand learning and development in higher education.

In this book I adopt what John Watkins (1964) refers to as confessional style, which he describes as "allowing the reader to re-think your own thoughts in their natural order" rather than "bully[ing] him into accepting a conclusion by parading a series of propositions which he must accept or which lead to it" (667). In other words, the words of the students along with my own observations are arranged to unfold as a story, allowing for considerable leeway in the readers' interpretations; allowing the reader, in Goethe's words, to discover "in their own way what has already been discovered" (Goethe to Karl Knebel, quoted in Steiner 2000).

This book is organized into four parts. Part 1, "The Inception," covers the organizational work and the first three days of the simulation, when the students were mastering the tools and the ways of their different cultures. Part 2, "First Encounters, First Crimes," chronicles our initial attempts at cross-cultural activities and the illicit behaviors the participants used in their efforts to gain the upper hand in the cultural game we were playing. Part 3, "The Justification," describes the final days of the simulation when the members of each group became convinced of their own superiority and blinded to any outside interpretation of their own actions. Part 4, "The Un-reconciliation," tells of our unsuccessful attempts to reunite the class as one community of learners who had shared a simulated cultural experience. We had imagined a four-week aftermath, collectively marveling at the phenomenon we had created together. Instead, our efforts at reconciliation further polarized the groups and the group leaders alike. If we learned nothing else, we are all now certain that we did indeed create two distinct cultural groups and that cultural boundaries are far easier to construct and fortify than they are to negotiate or tear down.

PART 1

The Inception

The Groundwork

At the heart of this work is the notion of a coconstitutive relationship between people and culture. In living our everyday lives, we create our cultural worlds even as we become part of them. Normally we go about this process unaware, but I wanted us to "do culture" in a conscious way and to document the genesis of culture, providing a rich, theoretically informed, multiperspectival account of the process.

I found myself in the fortunate position of designing my dissertation research during the same time period when I was planning the curriculum for an upcoming university course on cross-cultural communication. Looking over the syllabi of the other courses my prospective students were taking in the department, I saw that the students were inundated with literature showing the extent to which they were *products* of culture, but they were exposed to very little showing how their own everyday human activities *produce* culture. Culture is a two-way process, but we were telling only half the story, the half that ignores the generative roles each of us plays. I decided to interlace my research and teaching goals by designing a research project that included my undergraduate students as fully complicit coresearchers. I hoped to demonstrate to my students that in carrying out their daily lives they could be powerful agents of social transformation.

Romantic Science and Participatory Research

Many of my colleagues at the Laboratory of Comparative Human Cognition (LCHC) and I follow a research and teaching philosophy referred to as *romantic science*. The ideas proposed by Goethe and elaborated by those for whom romantic science provides a guide to educational practice are my major inspiration. Goethe formulated a mode of scientific inquiry that consciously incorporates the "metamorphosis of the scientist" into our understanding of the process of scientific discovery (Amrine 1998, 34). Goethe saw scientific experiments not as isolatable sources of knowledge but as artistic practices through which our "organs of perception" are developed and refined over time (Amrine and Zucker 1987, 187).

Romantic science is defined by its method of research and by the kinds of knowledge or experiences this method may produce. Scientific discovery is understood as the product of a collaborative relationship with nature— of a sympathetic participation in the development of natural phenomena (Zajonc 1998). The underlying premise is that a thoughtful observer, who stays with a phenomenon as it develops over time, cannot help but develop in concert with it. This synchronous development orients and hones the researcher's perceptive capabilities. The romantic classroom positions the students as researchers, allowing for qualitatively different learning experiences from those possible in a traditional classroom. The students come away with a scientific knowing as opposed to a collection of facts.

Rudolf Steiner, in his interpretations of Goethe's scientific writings, established the theoretical foundations for what was then a radical form of education (Steiner 1968). Steiner's vision, manifest today in the Waldorf School model (Petrash 2002; Barnes 1980), builds on the idea of participatory research, where learners embark on a journey of discovery, entering into the dynamic processes they are trying to understand. Instead of critiquing scientific hypotheses conceived by others, students of romantic science undertake a series of experiments ordered in such a way that, on their completion, the underlying ideas become intuitive (Steiner 1968).

The Research Design

My first task was to create a medium in which cultural genesis could occur under conditions that would permit observation and scrutiny. I needed a procedure that could be accomplished inside the ten-week academic term, and one that would provide enough "play," in two senses of the word, to allow culture to emerge as naturally as possible. The medium I developed should include play, in the sense of voluntary participation in fun activities with quirky or problematic situations that might promote creative thinking. It should also include play, in the sense of slippage or space where these creative solutions might take root and develop. The best way I knew to submerge people in play was to engage them in a game (see Barab, Gresalfi, and Ingram-Goble 2010). Games provide people with legitimate roles inside group activities, where their actions have perceivable effects on the outcome. Games direct players' attention to relevant tasks or events and provide the necessary concepts or tools to successfully take part; and, importantly for my purposes, games often stimulate conversation. A social simulation, a very particular sort of game, does even more. A social simulation brings people together in working relationships where players are affectively engaged and perceive themselves as having central roles in a developing story.

I searched for a simulation game that would allow us to retain many of the elements of "real-life" cultural work, particularly, unscripted interactions among the participants, unpredictable responses, and the emergence of artifacts and relationships that would be free to develop reflexively over time. At the same time, I wanted a simulation that would allow me to manipulate its parameters and factors to make certain kinds of cultural phenomena more accessible for observation, and one that would allow for interventions should the games take an unwanted turn. Culture is messy and complicated. The right game, I reasoned, would impose a measure of structure, simplicity, and clarity onto what might otherwise be a nebulous undertaking.

The solution came to me in the form of the BaFa' BaFa' cultural simulation game, designed by Garry Shirts (1977), which has been widely and successfully used for more than three decades as a tool for teaching cross-cultural sensitivity (Sullivan and Duplaga 1997). The idea behind BaFa' BaFa' is to give participants an opportunity to experience cultural border crossing in a safe space, and to reflect on and unpack their experiences without the prejudices and constraints that real-life border crossing often includes.[2]

In the original version of BaFa' BaFa,' participants are divided into two groups. Each group spends about an hour learning a different set of cultural norms. The groups then exchange members for short periods of time in an effort to learn about the other group's culture. The goal is to learn as much as possible about the other group's values and customs without directly asking questions—much like we are forced to learn when we travel to a foreign country. The two cultures in the BaFa' BaFa' simulation are vastly different: Alpha culture is geared toward community spirit and sharing, and Beta culture is focused on personal achievement. This difference provides ample potential for misunderstanding when moving from one group to the other. During the simulation each culture develops hypotheses about the other, which are tested when the two groups come together in the end to talk about their experiences. While the game was originally developed as an experiential teaching aid, not as a research tool, it nonetheless appeared to contain the necessary "seeds" (a few simple rules and artifacts) for planting the kind of small-group cultures that I hoped to watch grow.

In its standard form the game is evaluated through retrospective accounts of attitude change (e.g., Sullivan and Duplaga 1997). The speed with which groups cohere and attitudes change in BaFa' BaFa' is remarkable, but the game's brevity, while hyperefficient for training purposes, obscures the processes of cultural formation and change. To address questions related to the ways that small cultures come into existence, persist, and are transformed over time, the BaFa' BaFa' time frame had to be extended. The twice-weekly scheduling of a university course provided the basis for thinking of the sequential class meetings as generations of cultural experience, where solutions to problems developed in one meeting could be accumulated and passed on in the next. I hypothesized that if I slowed down the simulation and let the two cultures evolve over the academic quarter, the participants would have the opportunity to come to a deeper and more nuanced understanding of cultural processes.

The rules of BaFa' BaFa' were few and easy to learn, just enough to deal with the situations that were likely to arise in half-day seminars. The rules so written proved perfect for my purposes as well, precisely because they were inadequate to meet the demands of prolonged social interactions. In a more extended time frame they would require embellishment and additions as the events of the simulation unfolded, allowing us to observe the evolution of artifacts and the process of social norm formation and change in situ.

The extended BaFa' BaFa' game also allowed us to structure the research in such a way that as the simulation unfolded, as situations and questions arose, the students and I would read and discuss relevant social theories, testing them against our immediate experiences and using them to inform our analyses. It also became possible for the students to reflect on and write about their experiences in weekly field notes and reflection papers. These documents would be the core of my research data.

Student Ethnographers

In previous experience with undergraduates, I had seen that asking them to write "thick" or richly detailed descriptions of their experiences, and, importantly, having them include personal reflections about how they were thinking and feeling at the time, provided a way for them to define and evaluate their roles in social interactions and to better understand the impact their participation had on the development of group relations (Downing-Wilson 2008). In this regard the student field notes become powerful tools for thinking and reflecting. Not only do they offer a recording of the daily experiences, understandings, and interpretations of an ethnographer "in the field," but writing field notes allows students to synthesize and organize this knowledge into coherent narratives. I hoped that becoming ethnographers and writing ethnographic field notes would inspire the students to think more deeply about the simulation, relate the events to their larger lives, and reveal more about what they were thinking and feeling than would traditional participation, note taking, and report writing.

Narrative Theories of Culture

Following Jerome Bruner (1993), Elinor Ochs (2011), James Wertsch (2001) and others, I find it useful to think of cultural genesis as a multivocal narrative process. Narrative theories work in perfect harmony with the foundational argument of this research; culture is a two-way process through which we both create and are created. In the authoring of our personal stories, we are also contributing to larger social narratives, which in turn have profound influence on the kinds of personal stories we can write.

According to Bruner, narration is entwined with and constitutive of human life. It transforms mere existence into human experience. When we tell our personal stories, our acts are put into relationship with the acts of others and become meaningful. Stories are problem solvers. Bruner (2002) writes, "[Narrative] is a way to domesticate human error and surprise. It conventionalizes the common forms of human mishap into genres—comedy, tragedy, romance, irony, or whatever format might lessen the sting of our fortuity" (31). Narrative achieves these feats not only because of its structure, but because of its flexibility. Our stories are the product of language, remarkable for its sheer generativeness, permitting countless versions of a single event to be told. Each version is particular, local, and unique, and yet can have tremendous reach. Stories bring us to life in the sense that we come to see ourselves, or feel ourselves, in each other (Bruner 2002, 60).

Our everyday conversations about fresh events, those stories that we create *with* others, are different from those we tell *to* others in that they are not fully organized into standardized narrative structures. Life does not unfold in well-formed plots with beginnings, clearly defined central characters, and tidy endings that tie up all of the loose logic threads. Instead, the collaborative narrative process becomes a creative space where life's moments are brought into the light. Interlocutors move freely from teller to listener and back again to provide the commentary and criticisms that shape the direction and content of the developing story. Storytellers and listeners, in the acts of recounting, interpreting, responding and clarifying, become coauthors in the moment-to-moment, locally organized, emergent narrative achievement that we know as culture (Ochs and Caps 2001).

In "National Narratives and the Conservative Nature of Collective Memory," James Wertsch (2007) suggests that we socially construct and actively maintain "schematic narrative templates" that help us deal with the contradictions of living inside cultural systems that are at once constant and ever-changing (23). These templates exert a powerful organizing force on the narratives we create, directing our attention to information that fits within their structures, excluding information that is inconsistent with earlier assumptions, predisposing us to certain conclusions. These templates belong to particular narrative traditions that have developed over time as the result of historical events that are specific to particular communities, times, and spaces.

Narrative and Identity Formation

One question we were addressing in this research was how we come to identify ourselves as group members. Ricoeur (1991), Gergen and Gergen (1997), and Bruner (2002) all suggest that a large part of identity formation is accomplished through narrative. They boldly propose that an "essential self" does not exist. Instead, we use unspoken, implicit cultural models of what selfhood might be to tell ourselves stories about who and what we are, what has happened, and why we do what we do. Our self-making stories accumulate over time and pattern themselves on conventional genres as we continually rewrite them to fit new circumstances. Bruner (2002, 78) puts it like this:

> A self-making narrative is something of a balancing act. It must, on the one hand, create a powerful conviction of autonomy, that one has a will of one's own, a certain freedom of choice, a degree of possibility. But it must also relate the self to a world of others—to friends and family, to institutions, to the past, to reference groups. But the commitment to others that is implicit in relating oneself to others of course limits our autonomy. We seem virtually unable to live without both, autonomy and commitment, and our lives strive to balance the two. So do the narratives we tell ourselves.

Paul Ricoeur (1991) suggests that through the construction of narratives we reinterpret our identities within social, cultural, and historical contexts. Narratives work to synchronize ideologies and power relations, defining what identities may be possible within a given cultural context. Through narrative we find voice and agency, which Ricoeur calls the ability to emplot (32). He holds emplotment, or the authoring of our own roles in the many unfolding narratives that we will take part in over our lifetime, as the central process in identity formation and maintenance. Through emplotment, we shape our identity and the ways in which selfhood is expressed (Ricoeur 1991).

Narrative Manages the Temporal Dimension of Life

We use narrative to situate our simulation in time and to author our world as it emerges from the past, unfolds in the present, and moves into the future. Bruner describes the process like this: "We seem to have no other way of describing 'lived time' save in the form of a narrative. Which is not to say that there are not other temporal forms that can be imposed on the experience of time, but none of them succeeds in capturing the sense of lived time: not clock or calendrical time forms, not serial or cyclical orders, not any of these. It is a thesis that will be familiar to many of you, for it has been most recently and powerfully argued by Paul Ricoeur (1984)" (Bruner 2004, 692).

In telling our stories, we are not only recounting the important events in our lives but also making meaning of these events and, importantly, integrating the past (in the form of cultural-historical memories and norms) and the future (in terms of what we believe is probable or possible) into our understanding of current events to inform our immediate decisions (Abbott 2005). Social scientists refer to this process as prolepsis, "a cultural mechanism that brings the future into the present" (Cole 1996). Against a backdrop of history, we forecast the future, and from this construal we formulate our plans of action for today. Bruner (2002) says storytelling is forever in the now, at center stage, a dialect between the comfort of the familiar past and the allure of a possible future.

Ochs and Capps (2001) argue that the tension between the desire to construct a seamless storyline and the desire to capture the meaning and complexity of our lives drives our impulse to narrate. In multivocal narration our stories are held in suspension among the narrators and between these two imperatives, repeatedly subjected to scrutiny, negotiation, and compromise, until satisfactory understandings are achieved. Presents are turned into pasts, these pasts are used to predict the future, and a single line of development emerges from multiple possibilities. According to Morson (1994, 6) "Alternatives once visible disappear from view and an anachronistic sense of the past surreptitiously infects our understanding."

Multilevel Narratives

The coconstructive processes of personal and collaborative narration take place on multiple levels—from small-group interactions like the family units studied by Elinor Ochs and her colleagues, to the "nation creation" that is the focus of Homi Bhabha's (1994) work. Ochs and Capps (2001, 57–58) discuss the communicative means through which small groups of people construct shared systems of meaning making: "Everyday conversational narratives realize an essential function of narrative: a vernacular, interactional forum for ordering, explaining, and otherwise taking a position on experience. People apprehend their lives through the filter of narrative and build communities through the co-authoring of narrative; inversely, collaborative probing and redrafting of events propels, shapes, and keeps narratives alive."

Bhabha (1994), on the other hand, stresses those narrative strategies that shape individuals into cultural beings and constitute "the nation" as a whole. He draws our attention to the moment-by-moment performances of culture, which are carried along by, and interpreted within, the tide of culture as it surges through time. "The scraps, patches and rags of daily life must be repeatedly turned into the signs of a coherent national culture, while the very act of narrative performance interpolates a growing circle of national subjects. In the production of nation as narration, there is a split between the continuist, accumulative temporality of the pedagogical, and the repetitious, recursive strategy of the performance. It is through this process of splitting that the conceptual ambivalence of modern society becomes the site of writing the nation" (Bhabha 1994, 145–46).

What Bhabha refers to as the "performative" and the "pedagogical" work together, or infer each other, in a manner that is reminiscent of Clifford Geertz's (1973) classic story of Javanese village life where the cultural current, or the moral and aesthetic mood of the people, is infused with the notion that nature is tremendously powerful, mechanically regular, and highly dangerous. Within this current, "right behaviors," like calm deliberateness, untiring persistence, and dignified caution are performed quite naturally. This leads us to think about culture writ large as an epic tale, which sustains the larger social norms that underlie and support an ongoing narrative process, which in turn recreates those norms in the telling of small day-to-day events.

In practice, narrative is a quest for meaning when experiences often seem devoid of any sense. Narrative is situated, at once shared and personal, and unlike a chronological listing of events, narrative encapsulates the player's actions within an emotional and moral framework, and so provides a glimpse of the larger social ethos within which the events are played out. Any narrative is incomprehensible outside of the cultural system that justifies the actions of the players. According to Gergen and Gergen (1986, 26), "all events in a successful narrative are related by virtue of their containment in a given evaluative space. Therein lies the coherence of the narrative."

Once again, Bruner (2004, 692) says it well: "The mimesis between life so-called and narrative is a two-way affair: that is to say, just as art imitates life in Aristotle's sense, so, in Oscar Wilde's, life imitates art. Narrative imitates life, life imitates narrative. 'Life' in this sense is the same kind of construction of the human imagination as 'a narrative' is."

A Meso-Genetic Strategy for Documentation and Analysis

The participatory romantic science research plan adhered to in this project incorporates the meso-genetic strategy for documentation and analysis proposed by Michael Cole (1995a, 1995b), an approach that provides a way for the researcher to account for changing influences over the developmental history of an activity. This mode of proceeding allows us, in effect, to look at history from both ends, by starting with the design plans and then documenting how the students and I interpret the events as they unfold sequentially. Each of these interpretations is differently framed, based on the information available at the time of writing. At the time of the "final analysis," when the end result is revealed to the reader, the narrative includes all of the successive intervals of interpretation with all of the many voices that enter into them.

On Nomenclature

It is my goal to faithfully represent the perspectives of as many of the participants as possible. In doing so, I have quoted often and extensively from the students' field notes and reflection papers, as well as from those of my cofacilitator, Rachel Cody-Pfister, to create a mosaic ethnography of our project. In an effort to reduce the confusion about who is saying what to whom, I've taken the liberty of replacing all references to the Alpha and Beta cultures with the names they chose for themselves, "Stone Soup" and "Fair Trade Cartel," respectively. And, to keep things simple, the participants are referred to throughout as "Stoners" or "Traders," terms that also emerged during the early days of the simulation. In addition, I have applied the convention of using different print fonts to differentiate quotes from members of the two different cultures and those from the research team. Quotes from members of the Beta/Fair Trade culture appear in this font. *Quotes from members of the Alpha/Stone Soup appear in this font.* Quotes from the facilitators (Rachel Cody-Pfister and myself) appear in this font.

April 1st: The Inception—Baffled but Willing

The forty students who showed up on the first day of the quarter had enrolled in a class called "Cross-Cultural Communication." The course was posted as an ordinary upper-division elective, with no commentary to distinguish its format from those of other classes in the Communication Department. In keeping with the demographics of our university, women slightly outnumbered men, there were two African American students, three students who self-identified as Latina, and the remainder were divided equally between those of Anglo and Asian heritage. Once the students settled they were told they would be participating in a project that was experimental on many interacting levels. Not only would their activities in the class be the subject of our investigation, but they too were to become researchers, embedded ethnographers writing field notes from within a simulated culture, which they were going to create. The students were told that the experiences that had been arranged for them in the first half of the quarter were to be the foundation for the theoretical work that would come later. They were asked to suspend their disbelief for a while and jump into the project whole-heartedly, even though some of the class activities would seem strange, silly even, and their value would not be immediately discernible.

The group was given brief instructions for writing ethnographic field notes and the details necessary for submitting them to our online database. The students were then asked to draw a slip of paper from a hat. Each of the slips was printed with one of two versions of the following message: "Congratulations! You will be participating in the ALPHA (or BETA) condition of our cultural simulation. Please report to the Media Center and Communication Building room 103 (or 201) at 8:00 A.M. on Thursday, April 3rd." The two newly formed groups were asked to refrain from socializing with each other, and the class was dismissed.

It took many of the students a while to get up and leave. For a few minutes more than half of them just sat at their desks, looking at us expectantly—as if they believed more must follow. The first batch of field notes, based on this brief introduction, revealed that the students were simply baffled, feeling they had too little information to proceed, but too confused to even formulate questions. Surprisingly, no one dropped the class. If nothing else, we had tweaked their curiosity.

Below is a sample of inception-day field notes:

"I have to admit that the acting childish and playing games does concern me a little. It seems like it would be weird acting like this especially in front of other students that I don't really know. I am not sure how such rudimentary child games or systems will be able to provide any revolutionary data or results, but I am willing to follow the rules of the game and try to help out with providing the results we are seeking. I am curious to see the data post-experiment and see what kinds of cultural differences and traits are being studied as I currently have no idea." (Sam)

"I did not know what I was getting myself into when I signed up for this class. The title of this course, "Cross-Cultural Communication," seemed fairly interesting in that I had originally thought this course would be to study groups of people and compare how people of different cultures interacted and were integrated together. However, I did not expect the subjects being studied would be us! I am excited, yet skeptical at the same time because I do not know how it is going to work out." (Bailey)

"This class took me totally by surprise! I walked into what I thought would be a more traditional learning environment where books would be our primary source of material; however I am very refreshed by the hands on approach that will be guiding our experience. We will become immersed and be the culture that we will be studying. . . . I am definitely looking forward to this new and unconventional approach, but I am still leery about how completely

different this is to what I have been used to during my 14 years of schooling."
(Dennis)

April 3rd: The Origins of Culture—Hemp Seeds or Nest Eggs?

Frederic Bartlett (1932) established a precedent for using multivocal narration as a research tool for better understanding cultural production. He explored the nature of narrative construction by observing the oral passing of stories from one narrator to another. Bartlett wrote that the acquisition of socially constructed narratives is always grounded in an initial affective experience, and that this first impression results in an aligning attitude or perspective that is difficult, if not impossible, to erase. He found that stories were immediately labeled with an "atmosphere of attitude," which he dubbed "affective determination" (80). In Bartlett's experiments this initial attitude set the stage for the first reproduction of a narrative and remained consistent throughout the life of a story as it was passed from person to person. In addition, Bartlett noted that, in every case, the original details of the story had been enhanced and/or edited by the subjects to result in a story form that could be "satisfyingly dealt with" (94) or fit into a format that the storytellers deemed reasonable. Bartlett reported that, in general, narratives were altered to create, or make more explicit, the logical and temporal links between events. The desired result was always "any form which any ordinary member of a given social group will accept with a minimum of questioning" (175). He took the predictable progressive changes in story content to be evidence of socially acquired schematic frameworks at work in the production, acquisition, and recollection of social narratives.

Bartlett emphasizes the historical nature of all narratives. They have no beginning in that each one is built on the narratives that one has heard or lived before and, importantly, on the attitudes or emotional states that previous tellings leave in their wake. Bartlett developed the idea of culturally acquired schemas to explain how groups are able to function as integrated systems, and in particular how they are able to communicate richly detailed, highly nuanced, and emotionally charged information rapidly and efficiently. Rumelhart et al. (1986) describe narrative schemas as multidimensional networks that include knowledge gleaned from all levels of daily experience. Schemas envelop information about causal, temporal, and spatial relationships and integrate attitudes, actions, and intentions as well.

These constructions are not readily available to consciousness. Instead, they become second nature to us, or as Bartlett (1932, 45) notes, they are used in an "unreflective, unanalytical and unwitting manner." We are born, develop, and learn within these narrative schemas, and so function inside them unaware of their presence or their power in our lives.

Bartlett suggests that the memory of a narrative begins as a whisper of emotion, like delight, disgust, surprise, fear, or anger. Emotion functions like a switch or a key, providing instant access to all that is contained within richly embellished schemas. For this reason I decided to furnish the settings for the two cultures with objects that would evoke the moods or establish the affective climates most likely to launch the two cultural narratives off in different directions.

Inventing History in the Classroom: Planting Schemas for Cultural Narratives

I was thinking about cultural genesis as a multivocal narrative process, and since cultural narratives must be historically situated, I knew I needed to provide some type of historical foundation from which each culture's narrative could develop. In this case, since the goal was to have the two groups develop along different paths, two histories needed to be established. To this end I selected a different historical legend for each of the cultures. These legends were chosen to resonate with the cultural norms laid out in the BaFa' BaFa' game. For the communal Alpha culture the folk tale "Stone Soup" was an obvious choice. Finding a backstory that fit the individualistic Beta culture was more of a challenge. Finally I settled on a tale based on the New Testament, "Parable of the Talents."[3] I intended for the two legends to serve as different cultural frames of reference through which the students would approach the tasks and situations they would encounter in the simulation

The groups met initially in two midsized conference-style classrooms on adjacent floors of the same building. Both rooms were situated immediately across the hall from a stairwell that connected the two floors. Upstairs, the Alpha group was greeted warmly by "Mother Rachel," who served toasted raisin bread and apple juice. The conference room furniture had been rearranged to create a casual and homey atmosphere, and "Good Vibrations" by the Beach Boys was playing softly in the background.

Rachel circulated among the students, offering butter for the toast and second servings of juice, and encouraging them to mingle and get to know each other.

The Beta group entered a "business meeting" conducted by Mrs. Wilson, the "banker." Beta participants were treated with professional courtesy, issued name tags, and seated around a large conference table. Self-service water, coffee, and doughnuts were arranged on a side counter. The students served themselves, found their seats, and waited quietly for the meeting to begin.

It was time to provide each group with a bare-bones history or "backstory" from which their cultural narratives could be launched. I hoped the two classic tales I had selected would exemplify two different sets of values and serve as ethical anchors for the two developing cultural groups. While I wanted the stories to provide historical seeds, I did not want them to overly prescribe or constrain the trajectory of the groups' emerging narratives. For that reason the two tales were pared down to one double-spaced page each, and the students were exposed to them only one time, on this first day of the simulation.

Once everyone in the Alpha group had been greeted and fed, they were asked to seat themselves in a circle, where they listened to an oral rendition of the following parable.

Stone Soup

Long ago an elderly gentleman was walking through the land of Alpha when he came upon a tiny village. As he entered, the villagers moved toward their homes locking doors and windows. The stranger smiled and asked, "Why are you all so frightened? I am a simple traveler, looking for a warm meal and a safe place to stay for the night."

"There's not a bite to eat in the whole province," he was told. "Hunger has made thieves of honest men. Best you keep moving on."

"Oh, I have everything I need," the stranger said. "In fact, I was thinking of making a pot of soup to share with all of you."

With a flourish the little man pulled a cauldron from under his cloak, filled it with water, and began to build a fire under it. Then, with great ceremony, he drew an ordinary-looking stone from a silken bag and dropped it into the water. By now, hearing the rumor of food, most of the villagers had come out of their cottages or were watching from their windows. As the stranger sniffed the "broth" and licked his lips in anticipation, hunger began to overcome the townspeople's fear. "Ahh," the stranger said to himself rather loudly, "I do like a tasty stone soup. Of course, stone soup with cabbage— that's hard to beat."

Soon a child from the village approached hesitantly, holding a small cabbage he'd retrieved from its hiding place, and added it to the pot. "Wonderful!!" cried the stranger. "You know, I once had stone soup with cabbage and a bit of salt beef as well, and it was fit for a king." The village butcher managed to find some salt beef... and so it went, through potatoes, onions, carrots, and mushrooms, until there was indeed a delicious meal for everyone in the village to share.

The following morning, as the traveler was packing to leave the village, the elders appeared and offered him free lodging for as long as he would stay—in exchange for use of the magic stone. The old man just laughed at their foolishness, "How could you not know? I am just an old man with a river rock. The magic is in you."

While the Alphas were listening to the Stone Soup story, members of the Beta group downstairs were presented with printed agendas. The first order of business was to read the passage entitled "Important Events in the History of the Beta Cartel" printed on the back. After reading, the Traders were invited to ask questions—none did—and we moved on to the next item on the list. The printed passage, shown below, was chosen because it stressed honesty, accountability, fair competition, and personal achievement, the tenets on which the Beta banking and trading systems were to be grounded.

Important Events in the History of the Beta Cartel

The Beta trading culture acquired its name from an important event that occurred over a century ago when the community's leader, a highly effective and respected trader, was growing old and feeble. As there was no clear protocol about who should take his place, it was decided that the three most promising candidates should be brought forward and tested.

Each candidate was entrusted with an equal sum of money and given one year to do with it as he or she deemed to be in the best interest of the community. The first Trader, noting a recent wave of concern over the dilapidated state of the town's bank, invested the entire sum he was given on the construction of a fine new building. He was confident that its imposing style and state-of-the-art steel vault would lure back wary investors and their nest eggs.

The second candidate was overwhelmed by the responsibility for such a large portion of the community's capital. She had the large sum reduced to the smallest possible stack of bills and stitched into a specially designed garment, which she wore concealed beneath her clothing day and night.

The third candidate, whose name was Beta, asked the leader to hold onto her portion of the money for a little longer. She began to rise early each morning and walk to the marketplace, where she patiently learned the difficult language of business and diligently studied the complex rules of trade. When she knew she was ready, she claimed her portion of the funds and, through careful but aggressive trading, made a large profit for her associates.

At the end of one year the three candidates were called back to give an accounting of the money they had been entrusted with. On hearing the three stories, Beta was judged to have contributed the most to the community and was named successor to the aging leader. She enjoyed a long and lucrative career as the cornerstone of the financial community. It is her seal that decorates Beta currency and trading cards to this day and her work ethic and entrepreneurial spirit that lives on in each of us.

To ensure that the students "got the message" from each of the parables, and to establish from the outset the practice of integrating the simulation events with the participants' larger life narratives, the students' homework assignment for the day was to write their own one-page story, either actual or fabricated. This story should capture some element of what they considered to be the "spirit" of their (Alpha or Beta) group.

While it was not true of all the stories, more than two-thirds of those submitted from the Alpha tribe told of events where people had come together to achieve a common goal that no one person could have accomplished alone. Alpha participant Vivian submitted a true story about being rescued by a group of helpful citizens when her mother's car broke down on a rainy night. Note, in the final sentences of her story quoted below, the explicit connections that Vivian draws between the Stone Soup parable, her childhood memory, and her own personal development.

When I was six my three younger brothers and I were in the back seat when my mother's car broke down one night when we were driving home. My grandmother who cannot walk very well and speaks only Spanish was in the front seat. It was pouring down rain and whichever way we decided to go it would be about a three mile walk to get help, and the twins were too little and would need to be carried. This was before everyone had cell phones and I don't know who my mom would have called anyway because we had moved to San Diego only a few months before and did not know anyone yet. My mom could not leave us alone in the car but she was also worried about whether or not she could keep us all together and safe if we tried to walk home in the dark stormy night. A man in a red pick-up truck stopped to see if he could help us but my mother was afraid of him and she lied and told him she was fine. When he drove away she started to cry and that is when I got scared. We all sat in the car for a while and my brothers were crying too and I think my grandma was praying and then my mom herded us out onto the side of the road and we all started to walk home. We only got a little ways away from the car when that same man in the red pick-up pulled up behind us. This time he had another car with him that was driven by his wife. The man had understood my mother's situation and her fear and had brought his wife along so that my mom would not be afraid. They wanted to take us all to our home but we could not all fit in the wife's little car and my mom would not hear of splitting us up so we all got back in our car and the man drove away again. This time he came back with his neighbor who had a van, and his son (who I think knew something about cars). He had also brought a can filled with gas, which he poured into our tank but still the car didn't start. It was getting really late and we were all so tired and hungry so my mother reluctantly let us go with the wife and the neighbor lady to Wendy's for some dinner, but she stayed with our car. I think it helped that the neighbor lady spoke a little Spanish and could communicate a bit with our grandma. The man and his son must have figured out what was wrong with the car because they all showed up at Wendy's before we were even finished eating. I have kind of forgotten all about that night, but my mom still talks about it sometimes, so I'm not sure if I remember the night or just her stories about it. When I heard the Stone Soup story yesterday I started to think about the fact that our bad situation that night was too complicated for one person to solve but it could only be solved if everyone did something. The man with the stone was kind of like the man in the red truck. He got a bunch of people to come together to help us. I think I will always remember that now and try to pitch in when I see people in need of assistance even if someone else is already trying to help out because sometimes we all need to be in this life together. (Vivian, SS, 4/3)

In comparison, sixteen out of twenty of the stories written by the members of the Beta group were accounts of individual successes against overwhelming odds. Bruno's submission also tells a true family story, but Bruno's slant on the events credits the happy outcome to his great-grandfather's "persistent nature," which, of course, is an admirable Beta characteristic.

I would like to share a story about our great-grandfather. When he was a young man he owned a salt company. He harvested his own salt and distributed it to local buyers in his home town called Mokpo—a small seaport village in South Korea. One day our great-grandfather took a gamble; he took his batch of salt on a ship with his workers. He headed to Incheon city—a larger seaport village in South Korea where salts were gathered and sent to the capitol city, Seoul. By the time he arrived in Incheon port it was night time and everyone else had already unloaded their salts and sold them off to the buyers. When our great-grandfather tried to unload his salt the workers would not comply; apparently there was a large snake lurking around the port and every time the workers tried to unload, the snake would try and attack them. The workers were too scared to leave the boat. As if things weren't bad enough, it started to rain. He had to be careful of the rain because the rain would dissolve the salt. Our great-grandfather did not want to go back to Mokpo. He stayed awake day and night protecting his cargo from the water and the wind. He was determined to sell his salt in Incheon. The rain continued for three days straight and all of the merchant's boats except our great-grandfather's left the port. The snake was still there as well, slithering about in the rain. On the fourth day, when the sky cleared, the workers could see the snake, but it wasn't moving. When they went to get a better look, they found out that what they saw was not a snake but a rope. The workers could not believe their eyes. However, misfortune turned out to be good fortune for our great-grandfather. All the salt that had been unloaded previously had been damaged by the three days of rain. Only our great-grandfather's salt was safe on his boat. The price of salt skyrocketed that day, more than four times the usual price. That day our great-grandfather made a large fortune thanks to the "snake" and the rain, and his persistent nature most of all. (Bruno, FTC, 4/3)

As these two examples indicate, the students' stories showed that they had understood the messages imparted by their group's legend, and that they were able to generalize these messages to events in their own lives. I hoped that the "seed stories" each group had been exposed to would also provide fragments of history that the groups could embellish and from which the budding cultures might emerge.

The next task was to impart a little bit of confidential insider cultural information — not too much — to each of the cultures. The idea was to introduce a few unique ways of interacting that could be readily learned by each group, but that could not be easily deciphered and duplicated by outsiders. One culture (Alpha) would engage in rigidly regulated social interactions while their "work" (a card game) would be simple and collaborative. The members of the other culture (Beta) would be free to interact socially as they wanted, but their work/card game was complex and competitive. Descriptions and instructions would be minimal, providing space for differential interpretation, elaboration, and evolution of the rules and behavioral norms as the simulation progressed.

"Yeah, We're a Bunch of Stoners!"

On this first day the Alphas learned that their society was a benevolent matriarchy where warmth, affection, and tolerance were valued above all else. Alphas were instructed to stand close, touch often, and show genuine concern for each other's welfare. They were never, under any circumstances, to be impatient, unkind, angry, or aggressive. Alpha etiquette required clan members to greet each other fondly and then move immediately into concerned inquiries and detailed discussions about the health, achievements, and wisdom of each other's grandparents and other ancestors. Polite Alphas pay full attention to each other in conversation. Newcomers wishing to join a conversation in progress should listen quietly for a while to be sure that they can contribute appropriately, and then wait to be invited before speaking.

Without fanfare, Rachel put her hand on the shoulder of one of the girls in the class and introduced her to the group as the Alpha leader. Rachel explained that, as the matriarch, this person's power was absolute. She was to be deferred to in all things and under all circumstances. There was no cause for alarm. An Alpha matriarch never abused her privilege. For the most part she participated as any other clan member—always putting the well-being of the clan before her own needs. Rachel asked the group what they thought they should call their new leader. Since her name was Chelsea, and she was, after all, a matriarch, the group settled on calling her "Mama C." Mama C was then charged with the responsibility of naming the clan. After recovering from her initial surprise, and following some discussion with the group at large, Mama C announced that "Stone Soup" would be the clan name in keeping with the clan legend that had just been passed down to them. Within moments of the naming, one of the other students quipped, "Yeah, we're a bunch of stoners!" From that moment on, the Alpha group proudly referred to themselves as the "Stoners."

The clan of twenty was then divided into four families and given a few minutes to get to know each other, to decide on family names, and to come up with family crests. One family had three members with ties to Canada and so called itself "Maple" and used a maple leaf as its symbol. Another immediately interpreted the Stone Soup mentality as "hippie style." They adopted the peace symbol and named themselves the "Love" family. The "Sun" family adopted the sun as their symbol first and then settled on the name, while the "Connections" chose their name and then searched around a bit before deciding on a rainbow as their family crest.

Without waiting for further instructions, all four of the Stone Soup families were observed standing close together, touching each other, and sharing information (actual or embellished) about their grandmothers during the time allotted for "getting-to-know-you" activities.

The Treasured Ones

While the family members were getting acquainted, Rachel circled the room and arbitrarily selected one member from each family to be its "treasured one." These special citizens, who were identified by long necklaces of shiny red beads, were to be carefully protected by other family members. Treasured ones were allowed to freely approach other treasured ones, but not to approach anyone else outside their immediate family. When someone outside an immediate family wanted to interact with a treasured one, they needed to ask a family member whether the time was right to do so. This was merely a formality, as permission was always granted, but an important formality nonetheless. Should someone speak to a treasured one without first receiving permission, the treasured one was instructed not to respond, but to simply smile at the rude intrusion and walk away.

The idea of treasured ones was adapted from the original BaFa' BaFa' game where the treatment of women was highly prescribed in one of the simulated cultures but not in the other. The practice was originally intended to increase sensitivity to cultural differences in what is deemed appropriate in mixed-sex interactions. My first thought was to dispose of this part of the game altogether. I believe women's roles across cultures are far too varied and complex to be addressed in this fashion, but the Alpha culture needed a repertoire of social practices that would be difficult for the Beta visitors to figure out. Reassigning the role assigned to women in the original game to male and female "treasured ones" in our extended version allowed us to normalize idiosyncratic ways of interacting within the Alpha culture and maintain the culture's desired complexity without perpetuating the myth that all "primitive" cultures create similar roles for women.

The Incorporation of the Fair Trade Cartel

One floor below, the Beta business meeting was in full swing. Students learned that, as members of the Beta culture, their worth was determined during the fifteen minutes that they spent on the trading floor each day. Little mattered outside of their ability to be effective traders. A successful Betan was honest, consistent, persistent, and able to drive a hard bargain. Students would discover on their own that time management was an important element of Beta success, as the more transactions that could be accomplished during a single trading session, the more opportunities a Betan would have for increasing his or her wealth.

Participants were divided into four five-person trading houses. Each house was issued its own account ledgers to keep track of business dealings.

Members were given a few minutes for formal introductions and instructed to come up with names for their individual trading houses. "Sapphire Exchange" chose their name because three of them had September birthdays and sapphire is the September birthstone. "Bella Trading Company" was named after the lead character in a vampire movie that was all the rage at the time. The name "Country Inc." arose because during an ice-breaking activity it was discovered that all of this group's members enjoyed country music. "J2HAD" were the first initials of each of the group members' names (two members names began with J, thus the J2). The other members of the Beta culture first called them "Jays-had," switching to "Jayhad," and then finally "Jeehod" before the day was over. (No connection was made to the similar sounding word in Arabic.)

Each house was asked to submit a proposal for naming the larger cartel. The suggestions that came in were "United Bank of Beta," "Beta Exchange," "Cole Group" (after Professor Cole), and "Fair Trade Cartel." The banker listed the options on a whiteboard and called for a discussion and a vote. Each camp held its own for a while, resulting in a four-way tie. But when someone pointed out that the word "bank" was not technically correct, the first proposal was eliminated from the competition, and "Fair Trade Cartel" emerged as the favorite. Once the naming tasks were accomplished, the four houses were summoned individually to the banker's office where they opened corporate accounts.

The group learned that trading success was to be measured on three levels: each individual's monetary worth, the combined assets of the members of each trading house, and the overall wealth of the entire Beta group. At the end of each trading session the banker would tally all of the day's transactions and display the accumulated totals on progressive line graphs demonstrating the relative success of the individuals and the trading houses, and the increasing wealth of the group. At the end of the fiscal accounting period (the end of the simulation), rewards would be distributed to the highest achieving individual and to all members of the highest achieving trading house.

Catching the Rhythm

We were fortunate that the simulation was a part of university life, where regular meeting times were naturally scheduled and paced to provide a foreseeable level of involvement and allow relationships to develop, yet not so frantic that it precluded a little contemplation on the part of all involved. We established a daily schedule of classroom events, allowing a natural rhythm to develop for cultural activities. The first part of each period was spent attending to class business (a one-question quiz to ensure that the students accomplished the day's readings, a short discussion session about those readings, and a preview of the day's simulation activities). Next we opened the floor for questions about the simulation. This was the only time during the class when the rules of the game could be openly discussed. During the simulation itself, the participants would have to learn the ways of their group, and soon those of the other group, as we do in everyday life—by observation, trial, and error. The students were then given time to "do culture," to practice being members of their emerging groups. In the future this time would also include reciprocal visits between the two cultures, but for the time being the two groups remained carefully hidden from each other. Time permitting, the last few minutes of each class were spent talking about the events of the day and planning for the next class meeting.

Living the Stoners' Laid-Back Lifestyle

Bob Marley's "don't worry 'bout a thing" playing softly in the background pretty much sums up the rhythm that emerged inside the Stone Soup culture. Stoners learned that theirs was a wealthy tribe. In fact, resources and money were so abundant that neither worry nor work would play a visible role in daily life. A large pot of "gold" coins was displayed prominently in the center of the room. Stone Soup citizens were told that they should take anything they needed from it, but to be sure and put back whatever was left at the end of the day. The hoarding of money, or any display of attachment to or particular interest in money, was considered extremely rude.

The Stoners' days were spent enjoying each other's company. The room that Stone Soup called home was stocked with "comfort food" as well as a variety of craft supplies, like rough woven cloth, needles and thread, yarn, markers, glue, and such, all or none of which the players could use as they wished. Stoners could eat and drink, play their card game, listen to music, sing and dance, or engage in craft projects, but they should never forget to value friendship and camaraderie above all.

The Work of a Stoner Is All Play

Stoners were taught a simple card game that used only the aces and face cards from standard poker decks. Much like the children's hand game of "rock-paper-scissors,"[4] different card suits trumped others, and winning was a matter of luck rather than skill. While there were winners in each hand, no real value was placed on these conquests, and no scores were kept. Money could change hands, but this, too, mattered little. The amounts paid and received were arbitrary, and when a player ran out of money others would push some of theirs into his or her pile. The game was a pastime, designed to facilitate friendly social interaction—nothing more. Storytelling, laughing, touching, sharing, and caring were at once the prime enterprise, the shared inheritance, and the emerging product of the Stone Soup culture.

It's All Business in the Cartel

While the Stoners were making nice, Fair Trade members were trying to gain the competitive edge necessary to succeed on the trading floor. Each trading house was issued five stacks of trading cards to be distributed among its members. The cards came in five colors and were each printed with a seemingly random grid of 150 numbers. A grave warning accompanied the cards: the trading language and the rules of trade that were about to be orally shared with the group were closely held secrets that conferred huge advantages on the trading floor. This insider knowledge was never to be written down or shared with anyone outside the Fair Trade. Any leakage of these details would greatly jeopardize the success of the group and limit the players' earning potential. It is important to note that no penalties or procedures for enforcing the rules were introduced or even suggested. This left the players free to create, or not, whatever sanctions they believed necessary as the simulation progressed.

The Traders learned that their goal was to create sets of trading cards that could be redeemed at the bank for $100/set. The completed sets were to contain six cards of a single color, having consecutive numbers, one through six. The cards were designed so that each was printed across the front with a 10 × 15 matrix of single-digit numbers. Insiders knew that the only meaningful numbers on the cards were those in the four corners of the matrix. Those four numbers on any given card could be any number from one through six, but all of the corners on each card would display the same number. Outsiders would be unlikely to distinguish differences among cards of a single color, and therefore unable to assemble sets of cards that could be turned in for cash.

A Secret Trading Language

The Traders learned that all business transactions must be accomplished using a special set of words. The trading language sounded complicated when encountered for the first time, but once the system was understood it was really quite straightforward. Only six words were permitted for colors and seven for numbers.

The card game that the Traders were about to learn was a lot like "Go Fish" and would require the players to describe the color and number of the cards they were looking for. When asking for a card, the first thing to do was to designate its color. Colors were communicated by using the first letter of the English word for the color (R for red, B for blue, Y for Yellow, and so on), followed by any vowel sound. So when asking for a red card, a player would begin his query with "Ra," "Re," "Ri," "Ro," or "Ru." The listener ignores the variation in vowel and listens only for the initial consonant. Numbers were communicated using the first and last letters of the player's own name followed by any vowel sound, repeated to create the number of syllables equal to the number of the card that was being requested. My initials are D W, so I would communicate the number four by saying "DaWa DaWa." The listener ignores the sounds themselves all together, needing only to count the number of syllables that were spoken. If I were to request a red five I would approach another player and say "Ro, DaWa DaWa Da." "Ro" (which could also have been "Ra," "Ri," or "Ru") to designate the color red, followed by the five syllables, "DaWa DaWa Da," to indicate the number five.

An uninformed listener might walk into an animated trading conversation, which sounded terribly complex due to the almost infinite possible combinations of first initials and vowel sounds. In reality, only thirteen different words were being communicated.

The trading language also included a few gestures. "Yes," for example, was gestured by touching the chin quickly to the chest one time. To say "no" the Traders were to sharply raise both elbows out to the side with the hands left to dangle loosely down. Traders were told that it was considered very rude and distracting for them to speak any other language or use any commonly understood gestures while trading was in progress. This limited vocabulary would ensure that all conversation would be confined to the task at hand, precluding the opportunity for personal discussions.

Following this introduction the students were given a few minutes to practice within their trading teams. After a few awkward attempts most of us picked up producing the language quickly, but understanding each other was a different skill all together, and took a little longer to master. I assured the group that they would have ample time to become fluent in "Tradolog," as one Filipina student dubbed the language, before its use would be required in the game.

"Ain't Nothin' Gonna Breaka My Stride."

The original stacks of ten cards that each player received were purposely scrambled to contain excessive amounts of some colors and numbers, and few or none of others. Trading involved striking deals with other players that would be beneficial to both or that would help both players assemble complete card sets. What the Fair Trade members were not told was that in the cards that were distributed to the Fair Trade Cartel, certain necessary cards (threes and fives) were extremely scarce. In the following days they would discover that the visiting foreigners were quite rich in these valuable resources.

At this point, with class time coming to an end, both the Stone Soup and the Fair Trade cultures were told, each in their own territory, that they were now equipped with all of the materials and information needed to fully participate in life within their simulated communities. They were asked to show up at the next class meeting prepared to behave as citizens of Stone Soup or as members-in-good-standing of the Fair Trade Cartel, and then dismissed with an admonition to refrain from interacting outside of class with those from the opposite culture. Passersby would have mistaken the departing Stoners for a group of close friends leaving a party, complete with hugs and fond farewells. The Traders strode out the door with apparent purpose and direction. Country Inc.'s Tim was singing "Ain't nothin' gonna breaka my stride . . ." to the great amusement of his teammates.

Those of us on the research team eagerly awaited the students' field notes. For the most part they contained the kinds of observations and reflections that we were expecting. It was clear that after this class, the students had a better understanding of the project, and it was just as clear that they thought of it as, first and foremost, a university class where certain requirements had to be met to earn a passing grade. Members of the Stone Soup culture discussed their efforts to "bond" with others in their group, but their reasons for bonding were all directly related to the course material. We saw little explicit evidence of emotional involvement with Stone Soup culture. Jaime's notes below were typical.

> Initially it was hard to get into this simulation. The family seemed a bit nervous as we all felt quite corny. There was a lot of laughter seeing as how we have had no experience with this before. I felt a bit like a fool. As we learned that we could all have fun with the activities, we eventually went wild with our ideas. We wanted to assert our role as healers! We wanted to call on the rain gods! It seemed like a fun travel back to kindergarten in exercising our imagination. The family was a great way for me to break the ice. But I am still unsure about how this is going to work out further. We heard a legend, but how are we really going to take this to becoming a part of our culture? We are inventing it, but when is the ownership going to kick in? When are we really going to be the Stone Soup and not just playing make believe? These are the questions I am wrestling with. This is fun and stimulating though, and I am interested to see where this will lead. I personally liked the family naming and the clan naming. I thought that this will help in making the culture and our family come alive and be united. I like thinking of our grandmothers as well because it gives us a legitimate history and adds authenticity to the past. This helps in not making this a culture we come up with on the spot, but a culture that has roots other than the present (Jaime, SS).

The field notes from the Fair Trade Cartel actually revealed more emotional involvement, but not with the group as much as with the competition. Students were intent on winning the game—for themselves. Sam's notes are a great example.

I'm definitely thinking I can hold on to my 4.0 GPA in this class. At first I was thinking about dropping the class because the introduction sounded like there would be a lot of dense readings and analytical writing and that is really not my strongest area, but now that I see that we will be doing competitive financial trading I know I am going to kick some serious butt. I've taken more business classes than most people in this school so I think I will have an advantage. I just hope that my group doesn't let me down. The other two guys seem like they will get into it, but I don't know about the two girls. I hope we can fire them up. The language thing sounds a little dumb, but I can see that it would be to our advantage to make the trading details hard for outsiders to understand. (Sam, FTC)

Overall, the students' comments from this day led me to believe that we had gotten off to a good start. I was encouraged because the Traders were taking to the competition so readily, but I was a little uncomfortable with the aggressive tone of some of the field notes written by members of the Country Inc. trading house. My own notes from this day include the following.

They [Country Inc.] chose their name because of their common love for country music, and I hate to stereotype, but there seems to be a good-old-boy slant to their comments already. Travis went so far as to write, "I think Country Inc. is the best group because we have the most white people, and white people are more outgoing than other races. This should give us an edge. We are a bunch of cowboys and we're gonna whoop A**!" Oh, Dear . . . I sure didn't predict blatant racism . . . if that is what this is. They do know UCSD has a zero-tolerance policy [for racial and ethnic slurs] right? Surprises so soon in the experiment . . . What will we do if gang warfare breaks out?

As you will read in the following pages, this particular problem did not materialize. Others did.

April 8th: Heading Off in Different Directions

Tajfel and Turner's (1978) classic studies of group cohesion[5] show that the mere act of categorizing individuals as group members is usually enough to lead them to display group affinity and in-group favoritism. Following his Robbers Cave experiment (discussed in some detail in pt. 4), Sherif (1966) also reported signs of in-group bias long before the boys had even met members of the out-group. But after reading our students' field notes, we still questioned whether the majority of the students felt any sense of belonging to their assigned culture. An incident outside the building where the simulations were conducted alleviated some of those fears, but ushered in others. As Rachel, the Stone Soup facilitator, arrived on campus for the next class meeting, she walked past a cluster of Traders. Rachel was surprised by their mild, but clearly antagonistic taunts; "oooo . . . here comes the leader of the Stoners" and "Traders are best!" Although we found this behavior a little unsettling, a part of me was happy to see these signs of group solidarity. Now I could look for signs that the participants saw themselves as capable of altering and expanding the introductory artifacts they had been exposed to in response to the demands of the situations they would encounter. I wanted evidence that they were feeling a sense of ownership over their respective cultures.

Stoned? No-Shows, Tardiness, Boredom, and Lack of Purpose

Despite our insistence on punctuality and students' understanding that there would be a quiz on the assigned reading at 8:00 A.M., seven students were missing from Stone Soup at 8:15. Five students would show up before the class was over, but two just did not bother to attend. For the "Sun" family this absence was particularly problematic; only two of their members were in attendance when it was time to move into the simulation activities at 8:30. The tardiness created another concern as well. The beginning of class had been designated as the only time that the cultural rules could be explicitly discussed. This meant that absent and tardy students would miss out on some of the information necessary to participate fully in their culture; tardy students might never become fully enculturated members of Stone Soup. This could seriously jeopardize the progress of their immediate groups, and maybe even the entire simulation. My notes from this day ended with the question: "How can we, in a culture that is intended to be relaxed and anything but time-conscious, instill a desire in the students to be on time for a class that meets at eight o'clock in the morning? I was sure the free food would have kept them around. It looks like we need to step up our game."

Field notes from Stone Soup citizens offered some clues about the source of the absenteeism. Several of the tardy students reported they were confused about exactly what their culture should be accomplishing and expressed a need for more direction. Their insecurity in class had led them to stand back and watch while those whom they felt "got it" took more central roles in the day's activities. These students' reactions were accompanied by comments from others who complained they had been stuck doing the heavy lifting when it came to keeping the activities afloat. They groused that the others were making little effort to contribute.

Rachel and I decided to introduce "citizenship cards," which provided a way for group members to "mark" each other following their interactions. We brought them out now and informed the Stoners that, beginning in the next session, each Stone Soup citizen would carry one of these 3" × 5" index cards with them, presenting it when entering a conversational group and collecting it before leaving. When one participant found another lacking in some important Stone Soup attribute or breaking from Stone Soup tradition in any way, they would mark the offender's card with an arbitrary series of numbers. If the person had performed adequately, and within the cultural norms, their card would be marked with an arbitrary series of letters. Using these cards, a player's reputation would precede them into every new conversation. Our hope was that this practice might stimulate a little greater involvement, which might translate into on-time attendance.[6]

Pumped! Present, Punctual, and Engaged

On the same day that Rachel was dealing with late and no-show Stoners, I arrived at 7:45 A.M. to find an animated group of Traders waiting outside the door of our conference room, eager to begin the simulation. As soon as the door was unlocked the Traders rushed in and began rearranging the furniture to create a "trading floor." Each of the small trading groups clustered in a different corner of the room. When doughnuts arrived the students quickly helped themselves from the table in the back of the room and returned to their corners without conversing with anyone outside of their immediate groups. Sam hurried in at 8:03. He was winded and apologized profusely because his bus had been late and he had sprinted across campus to get there as soon as possible. Everyone else in the Fair Trade Cartel, including Nathan whose comments are included below, had arrived on time.

> When I walked in the room today, everyone was already moving chairs and tables around trying to get it set up. They seemed like they could not wait for class to start. The general attitude of the group was very enthusiastic and was preparing for a great day. It was nice and sunny outside so that definitely could have contributed to the good energy in the classroom. Some students were sitting with their groups trying to prepare for the quiz while others were talking and joking around with the professor before class. (Nathan, FTC, 3/8)

In their enthusiasm to begin the practice trading session, the Traders hustled me through the classroom tasks and the literature discussion, which were the first items on our agenda for the day. Traders then finished clearing the center of the room and retrieved their sample sets of trading cards from the banker's file boxes. A small silver counter bell was introduced to mark the beginning and end of the exchange sessions. I tapped the bell three times in quick succession and announced, "The trading floor is now open." Immediately everyone sprang from their seats and the negotiations began. I was more than a little surprised at how unselfconscious the students seemed to be about using the rather silly language and body gestures that proper trading required. Rainn offers her view of this initial trading event:

> I observed the class for a minute or two, and it was interesting to listen to the gibberish that everyone was speaking. At times, it even sounded like adults speaking baby babble. The elbows up with the flailing of the arms to say "No" and the waving of the hand to repeat the card that they wanted to trade for was so silly to watch, but everyone was doing it and had smiles on their faces. At first it was difficult to understand the trading language, as I would confuse the color with the number that the person wanted. For instance, if I heard Wa Wa Ca Wa Ca, I would

think they were asking for White 5. I found someone to trade with, and I held up the card that I wanted to trade. I named the card that I wanted, and my partner waved her hand for me to repeat the card. I said it once more, and she answered with her elbows up and flailing her arms. After, she held her card up and named the card that she wanted. I had that card, and I moved my chin towards my chest area to say, "Yes! I will trade you for that card." Mike Cole had come into our class and had forgotten some of the rules and the trading language. I was standing right next to him when he got his set of cards so I explained it all to him. He actually had an "Oo Mi Ha Mi Ha Mi" which is rare so I traded a, "Wa Mi Co Mi" for the one I wanted. He really didn't care about making his hand, he just wanted to help me out and make my hand. In my mind that was a very important trade.

Trading seemed like it was taking a long time. I wanted to minimize the time for each trade because I knew that it was important to get as many trades in as possible in order to make money. I could not think of any way to do this that would not break the rules, but Bruno figured out a way of trading faster by holding his cards up and going through the stack of trading cards quickly and then answering in the trading language.

I was having a difficult time catching the other Traders' attention. I did not want to be rude and just walk up to them; I wanted to have a signal saying, "Hey! Want to trade with me?" I used the sign for repeating the card as a way to capture the Trader's attention. Also, since we could not say "thank you" or "nice doing business with you" after trades, I felt that transactions were not complete. During the trading period, I have to admit that I exclaimed, "I wish I could say 'Thank you' or something!" Aaron also agreed with this. By the end of class, we all agreed that a handshake was sufficient in completing transactions.

Throughout the trading session, you could hear others exclaiming how the trading language was confusing as times. Some Traders even counted on their hands (a No-No). Luckily, it was a practice session. I heard a lot of English being spoken, perhaps to clarify on the rules of the trading language, but I was engrossed in my own trades that I was not paying much attention to what was being said. The cards that I saw most people trading for were green. Everyone had stacks of green cards in their hand. I also was trading for green cards, especially Green 5, but no one either had it or if they did they did not want to trade for it. Trading ended and we put our trading cards back in the envelopes and were told that we would get new cards for Thursday and that Thursday would be the start of the actual trading sessions. (Rainn, FTC, 3/8)

The Sisterhood of Stoner Women Dance to "Beat It" . . . Now What?

Rachel was amused to hear Jaime referring to other females in her group as her "sisters." She thought this was an isolated case, but as the morning progressed she realized that the practice was common among all of the families. That evening two Stone Soup members made reference to "sisters" in their field notes, *"When Rachel started to take a picture of our group I noticed that Jaime was not with us, so I told Rachel to wait until our sister could be in it too"* (Ginger); and, *"My sisters and I were making bracelets by coloring and folding the Traders' money"* (Jessica). As of yet, no one was observed referring to the male members of their family as "brothers," nor was either term, "sister or "brother," used in the Fair Trade culture.

Curiously (because it was unsolicited), a number of female Stoners had arrived with artifacts, which they wished to contribute to the project. Some were small totems, a polished stone, a statue with two faces, and a clay whistle in the shape of a bird, all of which the sisters suggested were emblematic of Stone Soup characteristics. Others brought CDs or iPods with music that they thought would help establish an appropriate mood. One student choreographed a dance to Michael Jackson's "Beat It." Jaime comments on this portion of the day's program.

> Now we are learning the work of our clan (the game) and creating our history with artifacts. At first all of these things didn't seem natural at all, but it is getting easier. Learning to play this card game didn't seem like it would be that different from any other card game, but slowly it became a way to open the door for communication within the families. Asking about grandmothers and laughing over the deeply fabricated stories became a diversion and a form of connection. I didn't understand why the game had to be so simple. It just seemed like a game that would grow old really quickly, but because it involved other individuals it became more fun to talk. As it turns out, the

*game's simplicity made way for us to slightly expand on the rules. I was
initially unsure as to whether or not a Michael Jackson dance was acceptable
for our culture. Did pop music and music from the here and now count as a
Stone Soup cultural artifact? Did moves from the hip hop genre even contribute towards explaining our Stone Soup culture better? All I know is that it
was deeply enjoyable and that it served to break the ice between the whole
clan. I wish my grandmother had been there. :) (Jaime, SS, 3/8)*

The Stone Soup students worked at being Stoner-style polite, which
meant following the Stone Soup rules about how to treat each other and,
in particular, about how Stoners should "feel" in certain circumstances
(always calm, empathetic, affectionate; never impatient, angry, envious, or
aggressive). They played highly animated versions of the Stone Soup card
game, and, true to the spirit of their ancestors, they were unruffled losers,
gracious winners, and always kind to their opponents. Likewise, no special
value was placed on the clan fortune, which was spilled out on a central
table for all to use as they saw fit. No one made any effort to hoard money,
and several players were seen offering coins freely from their winnings to
nearby others.

The students in both groups had been instructed to use this day of
the simulation as an opportunity to practice and expand on the skill sets
necessary to function as fully engaged members of their respective "cultures." For the Stoners the behaviors they were performing had no tangible
consequences, and this became problematic. Most of the students had reported having fun, and a few commented that they were starting to feel like
they were creating something together, but others wrote they had trouble
staying interested in a game that had no winners or losers. One Stoner reported, *"I tried to remember that the purpose of the game was to spend quality
time with the others in our family, and I guess it worked well in that regard, but to
be honest, the game became a little boring. I was much happier when we moved
on to designing our family emblem. I felt like we were actually creating a finished
product"* (Chelsea). My hope was that these activities would take on new
life and become more meaningful once they were found to be useful or
necessary in addressing the situations that would arise when the groups
came together. Again Rachel and I worried that some of the Stone Soup
participants were not sufficiently enculturated. We were counting heavily

on the upcoming visits between the two groups to draw the Stoners into new "cross-cultural" activities that would warrant their sustained interest and involvement. We had no such worries for the Traders' group. "They definitely drank the Koolaid" I wrote in my notes. "I have never seen students this invested before."

PART 2

First Encounters, First Crimes

The Psychological Foundations of Cultural Genesis

Kurt Lewin (1948) introduced two ideas that have profoundly affected our understanding of group cohesion and that relate directly to this research. Lewin calls these the "interdependence of fate" and "task interdependence." According to Lewin, groups emerge not because members share common characteristics (although they may) but because members understand that some element of their fate depends on the fate of the group as a whole. Lewin (1948) shows that the most powerful bonds are created when each member's achievements have implications for the achievements of the other group members.

Deutsch (1949) tested Lewin's hypothesis by assigning half of the students in his university psychology course to small study groups and informing them that they would be evaluated according to the progress of their group—in fact, all members of a group were to receive the same grade. The other half of the students were also placed in study groups but were told they would receive individual grades. Over a period of five weeks, the interdependent groups scored higher in measures of cooperation, participation, and communication. The members appeared to like each other more, acted less aggressively, and, on several academic measures, produced more than the students in the individually graded condition.

In our simulation, all students were graded individually. However, the success of their cultures depended on teamwork. This research was planned such that the fate of the individual participants in the simulation wholly depended on their ability to function as a cohesive unit. No one student could create culture alone. Moreover, the extent to which each student's fate was interdependent with that of their teammates differed depending on which culture they participated in. In light of Lewin's theories, members of the more communal of the two simulated groups were expected to develop more cooperative, less aggressive ways of interacting than the members of the group whose ethic favored individual effort.

Deutsch's findings on academic achievement have been repeatedly corroborated (see, e.g., Rosenbaum et al. 1980; Johnson et al. 1981), but more pertinent to this discussion are the findings that the students in Deutch's interdependent condition "liked each other more" and were more cooperative and communicative. "Cohesion" is the word most often used in the literature on group processes to describe this form of in-group solidarity (Brown 2000). But what does "cohesion" mean, exactly? Hogg (1992) defines group cohesion in terms of the members' attraction not to the others in the group, but to the *idea* of the group itself. In other words, members are attracted to other group members *because* they are members. What they are like as individuals is a secondary consideration.

Surprisingly, similarity among members does not determine in-group cohesion. Once again, the most important factor is whether a group succeeds in achieving its goals. Anderson (1975) demonstrated this nicely by creating two kinds of groups, one consisting of people with (self-reported) dissimilar backgrounds and values, and the other with people who scored similarly on the self-report measure. The participants took part in a two-session project in which they designed a new student dormitory. The two groups, similar and dissimilar in background, were again divided into two conditions. In one condition (facilitated), each student in a group was given an identical packet of briefing and training materials. In the other condition (impeded), no two students in a group received the same packet of support materials. At the end of the first session, all participants were asked a single question: "Would you like to remain in your group for the next session?" The majority of the students in the facilitated conditions (85 percent) wished to remain with their group for session two, while only 45 percent of those in the impeded condition wanted to stay put. Similarity of background and values had no effect on the participants' desire to stay with their groups. These findings led us to predict that to the degree that our two cultures perceived themselves to be successful, they would experience increased in-group solidarity. It was unclear, however, what criteria the groups would use to make these judgments.

Cultural Genesis as a Meaning-Making Process: The Need for Closure

Leon Festinger (1954) argues that a fundamental connection exists between culture and the human *need to know*. What people want most, according to Festinger, is to possess a valid set of beliefs with which to make decisions and judgments. He points out that our physical world, no matter how elaborate, does not offer standards for validating our personal beliefs, attitudes, or opinions. For that we must turn to others. According to Kruglanski and Webster (1996), the pursuit of a common reality underlies most social processes and promotes uniformity in beliefs and norms among members of the same community. Kruglanski and Webster take an even stronger position than Festinger's *need to know* theory, holding that our desire to have answers is so powerful that any answer is preferable to confusion and ambiguity. They argue that our need for cognitive closure, or the need to stop thinking about an issue and move on, is often more pressing than our concerns for veracity or validation.

The human need for cognitive closure is implicated in cultural genesis in two ways. First, it fuels the process of constructing common realities; second, it is instrumental in freezing and perpetuating cultural norms or patterns over time. One process that the need for closure sets in motion is a tendency to eliminate obstacles to consensus. Kruglanski et al. (2002) designed a series of experiments aimed at revealing the ways we redefine group boundaries to attain consensus on issues that matter to us. Groups of strangers were tasked with agreeing on definitions of harassment. Kruglanski and colleagues found that when participants' need for closure was heightened (through exposure to noise and time pressure), they more often expelled or denigrated dissenters while positively evaluating the conformists who contributed toward the emergence of a group consensus.

Once a particular group attains and normalizes the consensus position, a number of processes come into play to ensure the continuation of this norm. One of these processes is in-group favoritism. The desire for consensus as a means of closure invests one's group with particular value as a source for that closure. Turnover in membership would weaken the group's consensus; hence the delineation and preservation of one's reference group takes on new importance. As you will read in the following pages, when group decisions had to be made, dissenting voices were often silenced in the name of expediency. Whether this practice leads to group cohesion remains to be seen.

In-Group Bias and Out-Group Discrimination

Henri Tajfel's research looks at the minimal conditions necessary to provoke in-group versus out-group behaviors. In Tajfel's experiments, groups were divided randomly (e.g., by a coin toss or drawing of straws); no social interactions, either within or among groups, were permitted; participants had no reason to expect to interact ever again with the others; and no instrumental links existed between individuals' responses and their self-interest. His results show a clear and consistent pattern. Subjects identified with their groups, preferring members of their own group over all others, judging them to be superior on all measures tested, and favoring them with rewards, often at their own expense. (See Tajfel et al. 1971; Billig and Tajfel 1973.)

Tajfel (1982) finds two characteristics of intergroup behavior particularly important. The first is that as individuals display increased in-group identification, a corresponding decrease occurs in variability, or a move toward uniformity, in the attitudes and behaviors of in-group members toward members of an out-group. Tajfel's second observation is that as individuals increasingly identify with an in-group, a corresponding decrease occurs in variability in the characteristics of the members of the out-group as perceived by in-group members. Moreover, as intergroup relations deteriorate, this phenomenon of undifferentiation, depersonalization, and stereotyping tends to increase in scope (Tajfel 1982, 13). In other words, as people come to see themselves as part of a group, they begin to think alike about members of an out-group, and they begin to think that all members in the out-group are the same. Tensions between the two groups exaggerate these tendencies.

Group Membership Is Situationally Specific

The salience of group membership in any given circumstance is important. The extent to which we conform with a group's behavioral norms correlates directly with our awareness of group membership. A robust body of research and literature on academic stereotype threat, or the tendency for students to perform in self-fulfilling ways on academic measures, shows that when students are reminded of their membership in a group, they will behave in ways that are consistent with public opinion about that group. (See Gresky et al. 2005.) In one relevant study by Shih, Pittinsky, and Ambady (1999), Asian American women at Stanford University were reminded either of their identity as women (who, as a group, are perceived to struggle in math) or of their identity as Asians (who, as a group, are assumed to excel in math) before taking math exams. When the students were reminded they were Asians, they scored significantly higher on the tests than they did when reminded of their identity as women.

Conversely, when we are distracted and our status as a group member is not particularly salient, we no longer behave in ways that are consistent with group membership. John Darley and Dan Batson (1973) famously brought this into focus when they designed an experiment focused on theology students at Princeton. All of the students were asked to walk across campus to give a talk. Half were asked to speak on the parable of the Good Samaritan, the other half on the availability of seminary jobs. In one condition students were told that they were late and should hurry over to the speaking venue. Participants in another condition were told that they had just enough time to get there and set up. In the third condition students heard that they had plenty of time, but they should head on over and listen to the other speakers. Along the way each of the students encountered a man slumped in a doorway who moaned as they walked by. Our common sense tells us that a person studying for the ministry would be sympathetic and helpful, and in the self-report questionnaires filled out at the beginning of the experiment, each of the participants agreed. But the results showed that neither the extent to which the students rated themselves in the "kind" and "charitable" categories, nor the topic of the speech they were planning to deliver predicted whether they would stop to help a man in need. The only predictor was how much time the participants felt they could devote without being late for their appointments. Some of the students, while reading their preparation notes on the Good Samaritan, actually stepped over the prostrate man.

April 10th: Entrepreneurs, Sisters, and Brothers—and Others

Up until this time, because the two groups had not yet been introduced to each other, we did not expect, nor did we see, much evidence of intense in-group loyalties. I was hoping the exchange of visitors would change all this. I expected the goofy language and trading antics of the Fair Trade Cartel to be sufficiently difficult for outsiders to decipher that they would both alienate and intrigue the Stone Soup visitors. I believed the Stoners would have an easy time identifying the Traders as "Others" and constructing an "Us and Them" dichotomy.

I was less certain about the Stone Soup practices. The behaviors that had been specifically designed to be opaque to outsiders were exactly the ones that the Stoners had not taken much interest in, and so these had not become regular parts of the group interactions. For example, the rules surrounding the treatment of the "treasured ones" had been practiced early on and then largely ignored. In an effort to correct this, Rachel met with these special citizens at the beginning of class and reminded them of their importance within the group. She also used the first few minutes of class, before the Fair Trade visitors arrived, to reinstruct the entire Stone Soup culture about the proper care and treatment of its treasured members. The students appeared to get the message. Mandy put her arm around Treasured Fredrick and announced, *"We won't let any of those foreigners get close to our dear brother!"* But Rachel questioned whether they could maintain these behaviors once the Traders arrived.

At the Fair Trade headquarters the Traders arrived to find their banker ready with an envelope for each of them containing trading cards, which they had practiced with earlier, and monopoly money, which was all new. The introduction of money boosted the tempo in a class that was already briskly paced. Although the Traders were aware that this was only a practice session, the speed with which a trade could be accomplished suddenly became a key factor. As completed sets of cards were compiled, students would run, literally, to the banker's desk and clamor to turn them in for cash. Adding cash to the game visibly upped the players' emotional ante as well. The politeness of earlier days all but vanished. Trading that had been animated and conscientious now became frenzied. I found myself repeating over and over, "This is just a practice session! You will NOT be able to keep the money that you earn today!"

Forward Scouts

About halfway through the class period, envoys of five students from each of the groups were sent to "observe daily life" in the foreign culture. These first groups of visitors were sent as "forward scouts" on reconnaissance missions. Hosts and visitors alike were advised to have no interactions at all with the "Others." The visiting envoys were instructed to pay careful attention to their hosts' behaviors in order to advise future visitors on how they might successfully negotiate their upcoming border crossings, but on this day no direct contact was allowed.

Rachel was surprised at how comfortable the Stoners appeared to be in the presence of the visitors. She had been worried that they would feel silly or awkward performing the Stone Soup culture for outsiders, but they behaved as if telling stories about imaginary grandmothers, playing mindless card games with fake pirate treasure, and creating jewelry from scraps of cloth were natural pastimes for college seniors.

The Stoners who traveled to Fair Trade territory were not as content. When they returned to their home base they reported having felt *"like total outsiders"* and *"without a clue"* as to what was going on in the Fair Trade Cartel. One student felt *"completely ostracized"* by the Traders, and another thought the Traders seemed *"cold and distracted."* Allie and Jason tell it like this:

> The simulation today really threw me for a loop. I thought I would be naturally open-minded and welcoming to the idea of a new culture, no matter how different they were. But this group's language made you feel instantly ostracized. It was confusing because our culture was all about inclusion. I could tell it would take us a lot longer than a few minutes to understand the ins and outs of the Traders' culture. I know when you first enter a culture other than your own, you're supposed to sit back and learn as you go, but all I wanted to do was ask questions because the simulated environment was so foreign. When we left the Traders, we were all saying, "our culture is awesome, especially compared to theirs!" There it was; the ethnocentrism I never thought I would have during this experiment. It is true though, from what I have seen in the initial observations, I prefer living in Stone Soup for sure. But who knows, maybe the Traders gets to play games and share stories too. Maybe we just saw the way they make money to survive. Maybe they dance

to Michael Jackson after the money making game is over too! Either way one thing is for sure; those dollar bill souvenirs they gave us sure make sweet jewelry. (Allie, SS, 4/10)

After our dance, Rachel sent my family over to the Traders' culture (to observe only and report back to the Stone Soup). Armed with my digital camera, and Vivian's digital recorder,[7] we all went downstairs to observe. The Traders were speaking different languages and switching partners constantly. They seemed to be discontent whenever they had no money, and they used what seemed to be arbitrary hand signals. They had cards to write on as well, but it was the currency they valued more than the interaction and friendship of their partner! The way they divided up the money into amounts and stacks also gave us the notion that it was more valued in this culture than ours. The gold piece currency in Stone Soup flows freely and without hoarding unlike here in the Fair Trade Cartel. The room was hot and stuffy and the people seemed a bit cold and distracted (even though we were to be just observers, no one even noticed we were there). We took pictures and watched for about 10 or 15 minutes when Deb thanked us for coming and shooed us all along, but not before giving us a parting gift of a stack of paper 1$ bills. Glad to get out of the little stuffy box room, we ventured upstairs back to our culture. When we got back, our group was saying bye and taking the Trader observers picture! It was very interesting to see how they were treated by our culture in opposition to how we were treated by their group. It felt good to be back, and we reported all that we had seen and observed. (Jason, SS, 4/10)

Fair Trade visitors to the Stone Soup had quite different things to say. They (the Country Inc. group) reported they had the Stoners "all figured out!," that the Stoners were "simple," "immature" and "primitive." Mikelle suggested that "our" (white business-style) name tags were much more professional than the hand-crafted hemp identification necklaces that the Stoners wore. When pressed for more details, two of the travelers equated the Stoners' communal spirit and absence of competition with a certain backwardness and lack of education. After some prodding they admitted to the faulty logic of this conclusion, but held to their impressions anyway. The following is from Travis's notes.

Now it was time to spy. Everybody but Mikelle took the elevator; she took the stairs. When we walked into the room there were four tables set up and there were five people sitting around three of them, the fourth must have been the group that was spying on us at the moment. I walked around for a bit getting a general overview of the room. One of the groups had a laptop on their table and another had a whistle shaped like a cat. They were all playing with cards; it seemed to be a single deck of regular playing cards. They were speaking English but talking about their grandparents and family, it was odd. The game they were playing seemed simple; the head (dealer) of the game would call out one card or two cards then personally flip over one or two cards. The dealer could look at their hand and pick the cards or just randomly pick them, then everyone else at the table would throw however many cards the deal had said down on the table, except they could not look at their cards. If the dealer had a black and a red suited card they would have to give one gold coin to everyone else that had a black and a red. But they would collect one coin from every person that didn't have a black and a red. The numbers didn't play a role as far as I could tell. They players were talking about family and what kind of soup they were making. We think "soup" must be a code word, but we're not sure for what. One of the tables blew the whistle and then that table split up and joined the other two tables, increasing the size to seven and eight. The table I was watching started to play "Good Vibrations" by the Beach Boys because "it would be more fun to play and listen to music." One of the players had a nametag on, it said Phoebe and hung around her neck by a hemp like material, I couldn't really get that close of a look. Each table had one person that wore a red necklace with a pepper on it. Our group had figured that it meant that this person was the leader. We took some pictures and Tyler stole one of their gold coins. I watched a little longer making sure that we figured out the rules of the game and I'm pretty sure we had it right, because it just was not that difficult. Overall their culture seemed pretty ordinary and boring compared to ours. As we were leaving their teacher took a group picture of us, then at 9:00 we left. (Travis, FTC, 4/10)

The visitors' stories meshed perfectly with those of their hosts. Stone Soup hosts reported being *"sad"* or frustrated about not being able to interact with the Trading visitors, *"because we wanted to make them feel welcome."* Rachel noted that after the visiting Stone Soup family returned from their little excursion to the Fair Trade, they seemed unsure about how to mingle again with their own culture. The returning students sat around a corner table while the other families convened at the front of the class. Two of the returning students eventually moved to be with the larger group and took part in a necklace-making activity, but the rest of them remained separate and isolated at their own table. Rachel comments. "How interesting that such a short trip (less than 15 minutes) could have such a profound effect— upsetting the relationships they had developed with the rest of the class."

Phoebe's report reflects the Stoners' efforts to adhere to the rules of the game, while staying true to what she understood to be the spirit of her culture.

> . . . *We were instructed not to tell our rules since the observers from the Trader culture couldn't just be told our guidelines for interacting. They needed to learn them from observing only. This was difficult because one of our sisters had missed the introduction and needed to be updated just while the Trader observers came into the room. Luckily, the Trader people didn't overhear our conversation. We started the games by asking about each others' grandmothers. When our group of visitors came back to report about the ways of the Traders' culture, they compared the interactions to that of a casino. They spoke about how they played something similar to "Go Fish" except that people would walk away and say a gibberish word if it wasn't right. Deborah was said to be like the cashier handing out all the money. This culture thrived on making money.*

Later in her field notes Phoebe revisits the topic.

> *Hearing about the Traders' culture gave me a wake up call and forced me to hypothesize what they would be like. We all thought that they would most likely be different from us, but the differences seemed like night and day. I wasn't sure if we could apply their values to our culture. I also am uncertain as to what we are supposed to do with this interaction. Are we to hear about it and then move on with our own agendas, or are we supposed to integrate their love of money into our peaceful culture? This seemed a bit fuzzy, but I am excited to hear more about their rules of logic. Their different code*

words seem difficult relative to our own. They come across as more complex in their game than our four card draw. I wonder if it is just because we are on the outside looking in, in that their language and customs only seem more advanced to us because we don't understand them. Could the barrier of our limited understanding be the reason for this more complicated interaction or I wonder if they are in fact more complicated? I guess this will have to wait until another day. (Phoebe, SS, 4/10)

I found it significant that while virtually all of the Stoners wrote extensively of their efforts to understand and get along with the Traders, many of the Fair Trade Cartel members did not mention the Stone Soup visitors at all, and if they did, it was to say that "we ignored them" or that they had just "gotten in the way of our trades." At this early stage of the game, the Stoners were struggling to understand their neighbors and trying to find ways to interact successfully with them. In contrast, the Traders' notes revealed very little interest in the Stoners or their culture. Instead their notes focused on how to perfect their trading language skills and develop strategies that would allow them to triumph in the trading game.

Becoming "Us"

The Stone Soup culture provided many more opportunities for open-ended conversation than did the Fair Trade Culture. The result was that the Traders knew a lot about their teammates' trading habits and attitudes toward money, but very little about their lives or personalities. Few Traders even knew the names of all of the students in their immediate trading group. In contrast, several of the Stoners mentioned that they were spending more time engaged in personal conversations with the other Stoners than they did with their friends and families. This familiarity with each other showed up in their nightly notes where they were, more and more, describing the members of their own group as being like themselves. (Whether they were or not is, of course, uncertain.)

It seems that each day the room has become more of a place of comfort and has a feeling of unity. Each day I feel a little closer to my group members on a level of friendships and interaction. They are no longer just other people in my class whom I sit next to all quarter and never interact or speak with.

But rather I feel I share a bond with them every Tuesday and Thursday for an hour and a half. I know that when the clock hits 8, I am injected into a group and in some respects I have a goal to fulfill as well, as others in the room do too. We are in this together. (Bailey, SS, 4/10)

Being a member of Stone Soup culture I have definitely come to love it. Stone Soup culture is about caring for one another. We are not concerned about money. I definitely love the fact that we respect and value each other more than money. Our society may seem idealistic, but I love that our time together is relaxing. (Amara, SS, 4/10)

The Stoners commented regularly that the other Stoners *"thought like they did."* This often took the form of *"I'm definitely in the right culture for my personality..."* (remember they were randomly assigned to these groups), and then the writer would go on to explain how everyone in his or her group was on the same wavelength about one issue or another. The Stoners also began to think alike about the Traders, making similar (negative) judgments about the values and motivations behind the Traders' actions. Writing about her first encounter with the Traders, Mandy from Stone Soup offers the following.

I refused to talk with them, feeling a bit intimidated and confused. I was hoping they would try to make me feel like I could belong there but their aggression and egoistic behavior made me want to back off. Feeling a bit uncomfortable, I tried to find the rest of my family. I was relieved when I saw Dennis. We talked for a while trying to figure out what their game was all about. (Mandy, SS, 4/10)

Dennis's notes from the same encounter show that he and Mandy were orienting in similar ways toward the out-group, and that this one interaction went a long way toward building in-group/out-group boundaries.

I was disoriented because I could not figure out their game and I was so used to being able to speak English and laugh and not have any pressure. Their need to win was more important than any desire to understand each other's culture. They were so focused and aggressive that I became nervous and frustrated. I was so confused because I thought they would try to help us understand, but they ignored us and I felt relief when the visit was over. When we returned I was so glad to be back home so I could share with my culture what had happened. I felt much more relaxed and safe. A great part of the experience was that my family stuck together because we were all alike and in the same boat. We also tried to figure everything out by collaborating and bringing our ideas together. We all agreed that we had lucked out getting into the Stone Soup culture. (Dennis, SS, 4/10)

The Traders' reflections made no mention of group solidarity. Instead they were all about the affordances that Cartel membership bestowed. Comments like Bruno's—"The rules of Fair Trade Cartel let us aggressively go after what we want and that's true to human nature, or at least to my nature"—suggest that it was not so much the group that was affecting their judgments about themselves and others as it was how they needed to respond to the situations they found themselves in based on group membership.

At this point in the simulation the students still had very limited in-group/out-group experience, but their notes indicated that the Fair Trade group was unperturbed by and uninterested in the Stoners. Not so for the Stone Soup culture, particularly not for the family that had traveled to Fair Trade territory. They were very vocal about their distress and were planting seeds of concern, even dread, in the minds of their people. After a few conversations with them, Professor Mike diagnosed the Stoners as victims of culture shock.

I had been caught off guard when Trader Tyler stole a gold coin from the Stoners during his observation-only visit of the previous session. I was thankful that Tyler had revealed the stolen coin during the last five minutes of class because this meant I was not obliged to deal with the issue before thinking it through with my colleagues. Luckily we had two days to read the students' field notes and to formulate a plan for going forward. Apparently, the Stoners who witnessed the crime were also unsure about how to proceed. They had remained silent until Tyler and his team had left the premises, and even then had been reticent about reporting the incident to Rachel—not wanting to get anyone in trouble. Contrast this with Tyler's jubilant account of the event.

I think that our society will definitely have the upper hand. I was a spy for the first group. It was so easy to figure out things of the other culture. I even got to steal another dollar from them (doubloon?). They were very immature compared to our culture. They spoke English, and I don't think they are very into the project. I will be able to crack them within two weeks. (Tyler, FTC, 4/10)

A Thief in Our Midst

I was speechless when, just before class was dismissed, Tyler from Country Inc. showed off a gold coin that he had surreptitiously pocketed during his visit to Stone Soup territory. While his team seemed supportive of the theft, the larger cartel was at first silent and then disapproving. The general consensus was that stealing was simply not compatible with the underlying ethics of the Fair Trade Cartel. Because the class period had come to an end, the subject did not get the airing it deserved, and we decided to address the incident and how to deal with the offender at our next meeting.

We had expected certain infractions to occur. Actually, we hoped they would occur so that we could witness how the groups formed and enforced rules. The research team had spoken before the simulation began about leaving the students to do their own policing and penalizing within their groups, but we had not anticipated any cross-cultural crimes. Now we agreed that the theft afforded an unexpected opportunity for us to observe any differences in the ways the two groups addressed a sticky moral issue. We decided that Rachel and I would open the subject for discussion at the start of our next classes.

April 15th: The Day Stealing Was Redefined as Exemplary Reconnaissance Work

Rachel and I arrived ready to face the stealing event head-on with our respective groups. For Rachel and Stone Soup all of our worries proved unfounded. We were expecting the Stoners to express anger or indignation and to demand retribution or, at very least, compensation for the loss of the coin. Instead, the crime appeared to be a nonevent. The Stoners listened quietly while Rachel read from the field notes that had described the theft and were immediately unified in expressing feelings of disgust and pity for the thief. *"If money was that important to him, well, let him have it. We have lots more where that came from."* That was it. They had nothing more to say on the subject and quickly moved on to more important things, like line dancing, jewelry making, and, true to the reputation all Stoners share, eating.

In Fair Trade territory emotions (in anticipation of the impending trading session) were already running high when I introduced the subject of the theft. Immediately, the atmosphere shifted from a state of high energy to one of high anxiety. Luckily a number of the Traders had mentioned in their field notes that they were uncomfortable with Tyler's actions, finding them incompatible with the Cartel's ethic of honesty and fair trade. Many had called for sanctions against stealing and also against cheating, which they described in their notes as secretly trading outside the designated trading period and using English on the trading floor.

I began by reading excerpts from some of the students' field notes aloud, trying to provide a balanced overview of their comments, and then I opened up the discussion to the group at large. A flurry of conversation took place before members of the highly competitive Bella team took charge. They suggested that the Traders' faced three separate issues: (1) How should the Cartel deal with a thief? (2) How should the Cartel deal with a cheater? (3) What should be done with the Stone Soup money that Tyler had stolen?

Tyler's team (Country Inc.) immediately came to his defense. Mikelle appointed herself Tyler's counsel and circled the Country Inc. wagons. The team began by expressing disbelief that anyone could see Tyler's act as a crime. Taking the coin was not stealing, they argued, but a legitimate part of the information-seeking mission that Tyler had been a part of. Tyler brought this point home by producing the stolen coin and turning it over to the banker, suggesting that it be used for "charity." One of his teammates quickly amended Tyler's offer to, "We want it to go on display to show other people what Stoners' money looks like." Furthermore, they pointed out, we had given the Stoners who visited us some Fair Trade currency to take back with them. Shouldn't this be taken into consideration?

Tyler sums up his response to the accusations in his field notes for the day.

It seemed just like it would be an ordinary day in the Fair Trade culture.
I then was shocked to find the teacher writing our discussion topics on

the board. The first topic was "Cheating and Stealing." The main topic for discussion was my stealing of the coin that I got from the table when I was doing spy work in the Stone Soup territory! Personally, I was kind of surprised to hear the others say that I should be put on "trial" for helping out our culture in stealing the coin. I did not understand what the problem was for doing very good recon work, and doing everything in my power to help out our culture. I would understand if I were to be put on trial for doing something to my own benefit, but the stealing of the coin was done in selflessness, and not for monetary gain. That is why I was surprised that it was even an issue, and for me to be questioned in front of our culture. (Tyler, FTC, 4/15)

Those outside Tyler's team were not immediately convinced. There was a difference between the Stoners going home with money that had been offered to them and what Tyler had done. Surreptitiously concealing currency that belonged to someone else and then taking it without their permission . . . that sure sounded like stealing. Two members of the Bella team suggested that Tyler be turned over to the Stone Soup people and let them deal with his infraction as they saw fit. They were the injured party, after all, and the crime had taken place on their grounds. The idea got a little traction at first, but then Harry, from J2HAD, objected: "Turning Tyler over to them will just mess it all up for the rest of us. It will turn into a big stinky international incident. They'll never trust us and we have to trade with them next week."

The motive for this argument seemed clear enough; their teams were still waiting their turn to visit (and exploit?) the Stoners, and they certainly did not want anything to interfere before this could happen. These sentiments were met with words of support and nods of agreement. That was when I told the group that, actually, several Stoners had witnessed the theft and that the Stone Soup members were unsure themselves about how to handle the infraction. Silence, followed by moans from all corners of the room.

On the issue of which culture should have jurisdiction, it was decided that the incident should be dealt with strictly inside the Fair Trade Cartel so as not to further disrupt the fledgling relationship between the two cultures. In the end the act was judged a theft, not a legitimate reconnaissance activity, and contrary to the Fair Trade code of conduct. Tyler's case, however, was ruled to have mitigating circumstances. While the group could not condone Tyler's actions, neither could they impose a penalty when the crime had been committed prior to the rule being enacted. The stolen coin was accepted by the banker and put on display, not so much as an artifact of the Stone Soup culture, but as a reminder and warning about the Fair Trade standards of conduct.[8]

Rainn from the Bella group summed up her interpretation of the proceedings.

> The discussion was about whether or not the person who stole a coin from the Stone Soup during their observation should be penalized. His group (his personal defense team) argued that he should not be punished because he did not know that he would get in trouble for taking a coin. They argued that he and his group should not be penalized because it was an innocent mistake. He took the coin to show the rest of us what the Stone Soup money looked like. The class eventually let him off the hook for stealing because he did seem to be innocent as he did not know how much the coins were even worth and he just wanted to show us what their money looked like. However, Jenn brought up a good point that since he did steal from the Stone Soup, the Stone Soup should decide his punishment. Deborah even announced that the Stone Soup knew the entire time that he had taken a coin from them. Another aspect to the crime of stealing the Stone Soup coin that was discussed was whether the coin should be given back to the Stone Soup or if we should keep the coin as a souvenir or for money. We decided that since the coin was already in our possession and we had given them money on their first visit to observe us, it was only right for us to keep the coin as a souvenir and not use it for an exchange in currency. (Rainn, FTC, 4/15)

Walking a Fine Line Between Cheating and Gaining Maximum Advantage on the Trading Floor

Once the theft had been dealt with, we talked about the other forms of cheating that had been mentioned in field notes. Certain Traders (no one wanted to give names) were suspected of making deals outside the official trading sessions. Others were accused of speaking English or using unapproved gestures during trades. Everyone agreed that the rules were necessary and that some sort of penalty would be required to ensure that the rules were followed. The problem was that the trading language had no vocabulary with which to accuse another of not playing fair, and English was not allowed on the exchange floor. Harry's account of this discussion follows.

> I would say the most pronounced feelings expressed by the students today were regarding the penalty of cheating. Everyone was affected because it applied to everyone, especially one member in the group "Country." This is because he was the cause of the first discussion (he stole a coin which is a form of cheating). I suggested that we should just take a card away from anyone caught cheating (I was later caught cheating for speaking English). We came to a vote, 5 students were for the card penalty, 5 were for the jail penalty, and 5 were for the fine penalty, and 5 were just for a warning. I never felt a higher level of group indifference (figuratively speaking). Some people were deeply concerned about the level of transparency of our culture, as reflected by their emphasis on sticking to the prescribed language and gestured during trading, imposition of penalties, and elaborating on what constitutes illegitimacy (I got the message loud and clear, as I was a violator of such policies). Other people just wanted all of the trading to be fair and square. (I am guilty here too because I got so caught up in winning that the rules did not seem very important to me.) (Harry, FTC, 4/15)

Bruno expressed mixed feelings. He was probably the most aggressive trader in our midst and clearly wanted enough regulation to allow trading exchanges to go smoothly, but he had also been observed doing a little creative interpretation of the rules himself. Stricter guidelines would definitely cramp his style. He made various comments and suggestions (e.g., to allow trading within the small houses immediately before and after the official Cartel trading times). The members of his group (Bella Trading) went along with him, but without enthusiasm. Members of the three other teams, however, were not intimidated by Bruno, and ultimately all of his suggestions were overruled. It seemed that while his immediate colleagues deferred to his wishes to keep peace, his power was ultimately kept in check by the group at large.

In essence our Culture wants to go back to basics, only be allowed to use words, and signs/body language taught by the BaFa BaFa audio recording. The system is based on the honor system. I do not know how well this will go, nor if anyone lost any cards. Because of the stricter reliance on the Trading language our group could not implement the "group trading" idea we had on last class—to me very disappointing. Like it or not being stricter on the rules does give everyone an equal footing. I like that stricter following of the rules gives our Culture its essence back, but on the other hand this does not seem to leave room for creativity and individual uniqueness. Hopefully the Cartel as a whole can come up with more creative ways to express ourselves and expand the language. (Bruno, FTC, 4/15)

Exploitation and Frustration

The cheating discussion was put on hold as we were expecting Stone Soup visitors to join in on the day's trading session, and we still had an important task to complete before they arrived. A large metal cashbox was retrieved from its hiding place under the table. With some ceremony I opened the box and gave each Trader an envelope with new trading cards and a stake of $200 with which to commence trading. For the first time the trading game was "for real." Today's earnings would count toward the Traders' final net worth and that of their trading houses. This new reality was immediately evident in the poised-to-pounce attitude the Traders assumed before the exchange session. The excitement was interrupted by the arrival of visitors from Stone Soup. The visitors' appearance also prompted the hasty departure of J2HAD, the Fair Trade group designated to travel this day. J2HAD was torn. They were eager to get into the at-home trading "for real," but they did not want to miss out on a single minute of their only opportunity to engage with the Stoners on foreign soil, where they had heard that currency flowed far more freely than it did at home.

Once again groups of visitors were exchanged, but unlike the previous day, these visitors were encouraged to take part in the activities of their host culture. On arrival each visitor was given a bag containing local currency and local game cards. No instructions were offered about how to use these artifacts, but the visitors were free to interact with their hosts as best they could.

While practicing their card game last week Traders had realized that certain necessary trading cards (threes and fives) were extremely rare. Now the competition for them was heating up. When the Stone Soup visitors made their first tentative efforts at trading, it was discovered that they possessed a large number of the coveted scarce playing cards. The hungry Traders immediately fell on the Stone Soup visitors, who were understandably intimidated and clung to each other in one corner of the room. The Stoners quickly surmised that some of the cards they had been given were considerably more desirable than others, but they had no way to decipher the characters printed on the cards to discover which were hot and which were not. Nor did they understand the spoken codes used during trading, which might have revealed such information. The Stoners became highly protective of their card collections, holding them so close that they struggled to read them themselves.

Occasionally the Stone Soup visitors would conjure up the courage to venture into the fray and try to strike up conversations with the Traders, *"How is your grandmother?"* In response, the Traders would bark something back in trading language, like, "YO! KaPa KaPa!" (I want a yellow four!). When the Stone Soup visitors, who had no clue about what was being said, did not immediately respond, the Traders would move closer and speak louder. "YO! KaPa KaPa!" When this did not yield the desired results, they would crane their necks in an effort to sneak peeks at the Stoners' cards. More often than not, this would prompt the Stoners to shrink back, clutching their cards to their chests, and retreating to the safety of their own kind. At this point the Traders, very aware that time was money in this game, would shake their heads in disgust and hurry off to look for the cards they wanted in other hands. The frustrated Stoners watched from their corner, more confused than ever.

Stone Soup visitors like Elliotte, whose notes follow, knew that they were being taken advantage of, but they were not sure exactly how or why, or what steps to take to prevent it.

> *The banker gave us some little packets, and there were many mini cards of different colors. Some Trading people came up to me, but I was the treasured one, so at first I did not talk to them. A guy wanted to exchange his cards to me, and he was saying something barbarian like "yaya... yiyi..." I could not remember exactly what I heard. Dennis had told us that the green and red*

are the most valuable ones, so I did not exchange those. Fredrick wanted to test out if he was right, and tried to exchange a red card for a blue one. Then the Trader guy just blatantly looked at Fredrick's cards and grabbed the card he wanted and gave Fredrick one that was probably useless. They are totally taking advantage of us because we don't know the rules of their game. (Elliotte, SS, 4/15)

In their frenzy to make profitable exchanges the Traders had forsaken all efforts to be thoughtful or polite. What was more surprising was that they were owning up to their bad behavior, but making no excuses or apologies. Anna's notes do a great job of capturing the Traders' take on the trading and the frenetic nature of the exchange sessions.

I was repeatedly asked by the foreign man with an ear to ear smile, "How's your Grandma?" I would politely just stare back and say, "Ra! Ah Mo Ah Mo?" And he would just stare back with a questionable gaze. So I turned around and "BINGO!" I thought to myself, another foreigner stood straight ahead of me with an entire bag full of nothing but red cards. Without saying goodbye to the annoyingly friendly guy, I charged at her and shouted excitedly, "Ra! Ah Mo Ah Mo?!?!" She tilted her head from side to side trying to comprehend what I was saying. So I repeated my question and eventually she grabbed an entire handful of cards from her bag. I was practically shouting in my head "There you go, now show me your card!! I know you have a red four somewhere in that pile!" As she held up each card I would do the gesture for no then ask her again. It did not take her long to realize the gesture I was making was no. Finally, she came across a red four! My eyes widened and the corner of my lips curled up almost instantly into a smile. I quickly held up a yellow four and snatched the red one. Without trying to counter my offer she took the card and I was off to trade in my cards for cash. Once I received my crisp new $100 and evaluated my new set of cards, I choose to accumulate the blues since I already had plenty. So, I decided to try my luck again with the members of the Stone Soup culture, my strategy was they would be easier to trade with since their main goals are to observe the Trader society. My thought process was they would be more into watching and learning from my actions rather than trying to trade with me. Unfortunately this trade did not go as smoothly.

I was down to my last blue card when I noticed the timid foreigner in the corner, and I immediately spotted the card I desperately needed in her fragile hands. So as I approached her and asked, "Ba! Ah Mo Ah?" She literally backed up against the wall as if I had threatened her. Maybe she interrupted my excited tone as aggressive. Peculiar right? (Anna, FTC, 4/15)

In contrast, Stoner Melani's reflection demonstrates the complex understanding and appreciation that many of the Stone Soup members developed for their own card game, as well as the frustration they were experiencing at not being able to share the finer points of the game with the visiting Traders.

The card game in Stone Soup is probably the subtlest instrument involved in the development of our culture. It's subtle because the strategy of the game is a reversal of the goal of a usual card game. The goal is to engage rather than to win. The dialogue that surrounds the game, the stories we create about our grandmothers, are the true function of the game. The game's simplicity set up a situation in which members are pushed to join in collective dialogue and not necessarily because it is already an accepted tradition for Stoners to tell stories, which perhaps influences the topic of conversation, but the limited attention that is necessary to draw some cards, compare them to the leader's, and pass in coins, creates a void in cognitive expenditure that is easily filled by entertaining conversation. A real understanding of the game is the result of our interaction with the other culture and the communication snags we are having in trying to communicate the values of our culture to them without directly giving them the secret rules. On many occasions they bluntly ask how to play our game. And because the foreigners speak English while visiting us we have to adopt other ways to guide their behavior towards appropriate participation in the group and the game itself. For instance when they ask whether or not they are winning the game or if the number of the card is significant or not, my family just suddenly becomes silent. The Traders' inappropriate behavior seems to taint the conversation. Furthermore, because our matriarch always wins anyway, most of the questions about the details of the games are frivolous. Even if they are told all the rules, they will never understand the "why." This is displayed by their fascination with the currency we use while playing. They either stare at the coins, greedily accept the ones we offered, or scoop them off our tables into their bags when they are leaving. This is not to say that the foreigners do not often participate respectfully. The amount of chatter and laughter that takes place during visiting hours conveys that they could participate well within our culture, but again I think that at the end of visit the visitors don't understood that this participation itself is the point of the activity. (Melani, SS, 4/15)

Out-Group Aggression, Part One: Folded, Spindled, and Mutilated

Back in Stone Soup territory the students were much more animated than they had been on previous days. More Stoners had arrived on time, early even, and had eagerly entered into the simulation, but they were starting to complain about how unpleasant it was to interact with the rude Traders. In the wake of the first visit to Fair Trade territory, the Stoners discussed what should be done with the Traders' money that the traveling Stoners had returned with. The Stone Soup did not need any more money. Other than its novelty, and of course its meaning as a gift from the foreigners, the Traders' currency had no real value in Stoner territory. Everyone agreed that it did not seem right to set it aside. Somehow, it should be displayed, as one does with a cherished gift, to show the Traders that their offering was appreciated. Jaime suggested that it be used to make jewelry that could be worn proudly by the Stoners or gifted back to the Traders. And so it was. The bills were colored with markers, folded into rings, twisted and tied into bracelets and necklaces, and shaped as feathers in headdresses. At first Rachel and I took these activities at face value—a thoughtful gesture on the part of the Stoners that was in keeping with their ethic of valuing kindness over money. Once the field notes started coming in, however, we realized this was a not-so-subtle form of aggression. Jaime's notes articulate the Stoners' thinking perfectly.

The souvenir of this experience was a wad of one-dollar bills, which were the least valuable in the Traders' culture. Rachel inquired as to what we should do with this currency. Knowing that it would probably and most definitely anger the Traders if we tampered with their precious money, I suggested we do something wild with it besides leaving them untouched. Someone mentioned using these bills as gifts to give back to the Traders, essentially giving it back destroyed to show them how little their money meant to us. This gift process then translated to a decoration party of folding and coloring the bills. In our table we did origami. Actually, after seeing what one guy did with his money, all of us at the table asked for a dollar-bill ring. He became the maker of money rings! Afterwards we colored the rings with our family colors. Other families made earrings, making use of the string on our identifiers. The less our creations looked like Trader money, the happier we all became. My grandmother would look so pretty in Stoner Jewelry. :) (Jaime, SS, 4/15)

The Stoners jumped whole-heartedly into their craft of folding, coloring, threading, and spindling Fair Trade currency in the production of jewelry, origami jumping frogs, paper airplanes, and various other hand-crafted items. On the surface this was done in the spirit of creativity and generosity; most of the pieces were given away to the visiting Traders. Underlying this industry, however, was the smug knowledge that the Stoners were belittling that which the Traders valued most. The Stoners had perfected the art of passive-aggression in a socially sanctioned way. A ritual soon developed; the Stoners fashioned treasures and "innocently" bestowed them on the greedy Traders; the Traders feigned delight and responded with profuse gratitude, before slipping away to hastily destroy the Stoners' handiwork to cash in the currency.

Fortifying the Boundaries

While the Stoners were busy crafting jewelry and fabricating legendary grandmothers, members of the Fair Trade Cartel were refining the code words and gestures that would allow them to trade effectively without giving away important information to outsiders. They worked at making these signs as difficult to decipher as possible. For example, according to the original language rules the colors of the trading cards (red, green, blue, yellow, orange, and white) could have been communicated using the first letter of each color, followed by any vowel sound, but in practice most of the Traders were using only the short "a" when designating red, blue and white cards, and the long "o" for yellow, green, and orange. Red was always "rah" and blue was always "bah." Yellow was always "yo" and green was always "go." Now they took pains to vary the sounds they were using, communicating the color red, for example, as "ray," "ree," "rye," "roe," "ruh," "rue." While the Traders knew to listen only for the consonant, they hoped that the outsiders might be led to believe that each vowel sound had a different meaning. They followed a similar plan in communicating numbers, in hopes of confusing the Stoners for as long as possible to maintain their edge in the trading games. The gesture for yes, touching the chin once quickly to the chest, was deemed too similar to the common affirmative nod of the head. It was replaced with an exaggerated blink of the eyes.

Out-Group Aggression, Part Two: I'm Not Your Grandma!

When the visiting Stoners left the Cartel and the J2HAD team returned home from the Stone Soup territory, I gave the traveling team a chance to tell us what they had learned about the Stoner's culture, encouraging them to be brief as we needed to return to the cheating discussion before the class was dismissed. Members of J2HAD were convinced that the words "grandma" and "soup" must be part of some secret Stoners' language or code—much like the nonsense words used in the Cartel's trading language. The following reflection is from Aaron's visit to Stone Soup territory.

> Semi-mockingly, I asked how their grandma was and what she was cooking. They responded deceptively and each told a story of nonsense. One said her grandma was climbing Everest and she was at base camp and how it was dangerous and a lot of people die attempting to climb it, etc. As the TA came by, a member of the table asked her how her grandma was and she told another unbelievable story. But it didn't always seem completely nonsense as one member (Japanese) mentioned his grandma still lived in Japan on a farm with chickens, etc. His story sounded semi-plausible so I am not sure if all the stories are completely made up or not, and I have no idea what they might really mean. For all we know the Stoners might be cannibals. When they talk about soup, they might be saying "let's have Aaron for dinner." (Aaron, FTC, 4/15)

The class agreed with J2HAD's assessment and offered a flood of collaborating evidence. Abruptly Harry yelled over the din, "I've got it!" Let's use the word 'grandma' to announce that someone has broken the rules. Whatever 'grandma' means to them, I know it's not 'you're a cheater.' That will really confuse them!" And so it was decided; when Traders wanted to accuse someone of breaking the rules, they would point at the offender and yell "GRANDMA!" Soon an accompanying practice was established; if the accused did not agree that they had broken a rule, they would counter by barking "GRANDPA!" Any witnesses could support one or the other by echoing either "grandma" or "grandpa," and if the accusation was upheld, the cheater would forfeit one card to the accuser and pay $50 to the banker.

The habit of chastising each other with the word "grandma" turned out to be a far more aggressive act on the part of the Traders than they imagined at the time. The word "grandma" was first used habitually in Stone Soup activities where it retained its conventional English meaning but was employed in very specific ways to help achieve group cohesion. *"How is your grandmother?"* was the traditional Stone Soup greeting, to be gotten out of the way before any other business could be attended to. Parting words always included wishes for grandma's continued health and longevity. It was also customary for Stone Soup members to pass the time telling stories to one another. Having just greeted each other with a reference to grandma, it was only natural that she would, more often than not, become a central character in these stories. The tales usually started out simple, but in an effort to keep things interesting, they became more and more fabulous as the simulation progressed. Thus it is not surprising that the notion of an eccentric grandmother, one whose escapades were fun to recount and could be counted on to draw appreciative or astonished responses from the audience, readily took hold.

Many of these stories began as factual accounts of the lives of the students' ancestors that were then lavishly embellished with each retelling. One Canadian grandmother, described as a retired second-grade teacher during the first week of class, evolved into a hippie living in a forest commune, singing, dancing and *"sending out vibrations of peace to the world."* There was an affluent Chinese grandmother who, in week one, spent her days playing golf, mahjong, and blackjack. After a couple of retellings, she became a dragon-lady tycoon who marketed her secret family recipes for noodles and oxtail soup and used the proceeds from her new business to fight crime lords in Hong Kong. The most fantastic story was about a Korean grandmother who, when first introduced, employed herbal remedies to heal her family's ailments. She quickly transformed into *"a magical medicine woman"* who miraculously grew younger each year; but when she regressed to the age of thirteen, she reversed direction, growing older each year, and lived on until, at the age of six hundred and sixty-six, she told everyone she had had enough and just sat down and died.

The Stone Soup emphasis on grandmothers served to link the classroom cultural experiences with the students' home lives and home cultures in ways that we did not expect. All of the in-class fabricating about grandmothers appeared to be stimulating a lot of real-life reminiscing about them as well, as Melissa's unsolicited add-on to her field notes suggests.

> *Being born into a wealthy Hong Kong family, raised by well educated parents, and fortunate enough to attend college in the US, my grandmother is a very bright, elegant, and sophisticated woman. Since she is the eldest daughter in her family, she has always been a great sister loving and caring for her younger brothers and sisters. She has the soul of unconditional giving and the heart of forgiveness. Her compassion is magnificent. Rarely will she refuse to help others, especially her love ones. She feels she has the obligation to protect her family and the responsibility to take care of all the family matters. My grandmother is very outgoing and family oriented. Every Sunday, she says, is a family day. Everyone in my family gathers together and spends the whole day with each other. Usually, we have lunch in a dim-sum restaurant and after lunch we either go watch a movie if there is something good showing on the Movie Theater or go shopping and then afternoon tea at the mall. During her leisure time, my grandmother goes golfing with her friends or invites them over to her house to have dinner and plays Mahjong and Black Jack. Her life is full of colors and excitement. Every time I visit her, I see a happy face. The only times I see an unhappy face are when any of her family members and friends are anxious, irritated, bothered, and pessimistic over the matters of money and relationships. Every time, if anything happens that money is the only solution to resolve the problem, my grandmother, without hesitations, gives out her emergency money to help them. When she sees her love ones are hurt from a relationship, she tries to cure them by manifesting the power of forgiveness. To me, my grandmother is an angel. I love her so much. (Melissa, SS, 4/10)*

The Stone Soup grandmothers also worked their way into almost every other aspect of Stone Soup life. When food was shared, whether it was Oreo cookies, apples, or tortilla chips, grandmother had either cooked it herself, created the recipe, or sent it along (from Tokyo, Taiwan, or

Toronto) with her best wishes. All of the Stone Soup's craft projects became reproductions of things grandmother used to make. Songs and dances (like the Stone Soup rendition of Michael Jackson's "Beat It!") had all been passed down from grandmother. Card games were played by grandmother's rules, and Stoner norms for polite social interaction were maintained because grandmother said we should do it this way.

We were surprised at how deeply the Stone Soup members took this part of the simulation to heart. As Sailer's notes indicate, the lines between in-the-flesh grandmothers and the simulated versions of them became very blurred.

> The other finding I got from this class is the memory of my grandmother. My grandmother died when I was really little, I barely know anything about her. However, many members from Stone Soup culture share their stories to me about their grandmothers make me feel as if my grandmother had the same characteristics or experiences as their grandmothers. By listening to my members' stories about their grandmothers, whether they are true or not, I construct my own grandmother in my mind by embracing their information. I do not feel awkward or uncomfortable when they talk about their grandmothers because my memories toward my grandmother are inextricably entwined with how the people around me feel about theirs. The reason is that we can understand ourselves only through our relationships with others. Even though everyone's grandmother is not all the same, I believe that the characteristics of grandmother, for example, kind and loving to their own grandchildren, are the same. I really appreciate my new "family members" because they help me to create my grandmother's image by sharing their stories with me. Therefore, I will not hesitate or be confused when somebody asks my "how is your grandmother?" because she IS doing well somewhere I cannot reach but she is always in my mind. (Sailer, SS, 4/17)

Now that the Traders had appropriated the word "grandma," it took on a totally new set of meanings and a life of its own. Once the idea of using the words "grandma" and "grandpa" as words of censure had been unanimously and gleefully accepted, it was not long before Traders who were caught overstepping any sort of boundary were labeled "grandmas." The habit spread rapidly and expanded to include all varieties of mistakes and infractions. When the facilitator forgot to bring in a day's quiz, when a student was unable to answer a question about one of the readings, or when someone accidentally hit the light switch in the windowless room, they "got the grandma word" (a phrase that featured often in the field notes, along with "used the grandma word," which was sometimes shortened to "used the G-word"). Spilling drinks and dropping food or game cards earned one-grandma status, as did losing track of time in the trading game. One (male) student arriving late for class muttered, "I'm such a grandma."

April 17th: The Day of Leaks and Lies

The Stoners were growing increasingly frustrated with their inability to crack the Traders' language code and to understand the rules of the Cartel's trading game. In response to the multiple distress calls that surfaced in the field notes, the first order of business in Stone Soup territory was to try and compile all of the information that had been gathered about the Trading Cartel and to see whether some sense could be made of it. The Stoners had decided that the goofy arm gesture, the one that Jaime called "spastic jazz hands," where the arms were extended to the side and then the left to dangle from the elbows, must mean "no." They also knew that the goal of the trading game was to acquire stacks of cards of a uniform color that could be turned in to the banker for cash. But when the visiting Stoners approached the banker with such a stack, the banker would look through the cards carefully and then hand them back saying, *"I'm sorry. This set is not complete."* It was suggested that the numbers on the cards might be important, and the Stoners who were packing up for their visit to the Cartel were instructed to pay closer attention to them during their visit.

In Fair Trade territory the Traders did nothing to make the Stone Soup people's task any easier, nor did they make any effort to make their visitors feel welcome. The two excerpts that follow describe the same interaction, giving us some feel for what the Stone Soup people were up against. The first is from Trader Sam, who offers a fractured account, decipherable only by those familiar with the Cartel's rules of engagement. The second is from a visiting Stone Soup member who had attempted to trade with Sam.

> The simulation began as the strangers entered the room and simultaneously the bell was ringing that says "the trading session is open." I conducted trades as before, but feeling more confident of what to do

and how to do it. The Trading language no longer felt unnatural (even with the addition of the words "grandma" + "grandpa"). I knew a blue 5 was rare, so I did not bother taking my nearly completed set out of the envelope. (Only to later realize that I needed them to communicate that I wanted blue with the strangers.) Before this interaction however, I recalled having horrible luck getting yellow or orange cards, no one wanted to trade. I approached the strangers and tried to communicate blue while holding up an orange card. The Stone Soup girl held out an orange card and I waved my arms while slightly nodding my head from side to side while repeating, Ba! Ba! for blue. I later realized this was a violation, and despite another member yelling out "grandma!" to which I instinctively responded "grandpa!" nothing bad happened to me. I later caught myself nodding my head the same way, and another Trader member yelled "grandma!" so this time I held out my cards and she chose a blue one from my hand. (I later realized she accused me of a different crime, but we had no real way of discussing this misunderstanding.) I approached another stranger once more, this time she said "how was your grandma!" I instinctively yelled "grandpa!" Jessica who was right next to me, yelled "grandpa!" coming to my defense, I smiled at her. The whole grandma grandpa thing seemed to have a life of its own. Then the bell rang, signaling an end to the trading session. (Sam, FTC, 4/17)

And now Fredrick's account of the same interaction.

Upon arriving at the Trading culture's abode, I think we were "buzzed" in after knocking or at else some kind of bell was rung announcing our arrival. Immediately, we were greeted by what seemed to be a banker, which I infer because she was dispensing paper money to her comrades based on some quantity of colored cards. All of us in the Sun family were unnerved and tried to stick together. They had their own language they used during their game, which was difficult to decipher, but I gathered that they had a basic greeting, different names for colors, and a declinatory gesture. If you didn't have something or didn't wish to play, you made a gesture with your arms in a right angular formation. Some guy kept pushing an orange card in my face and yelling bah bah bah. I thought he wanted my orange card, but he wanted to give me his orange card in exchange for something, but I could not figure out which card he wanted. We were met with some contempt when we asked the Traders how their grandmothers were. One of them exclaimed in response, "Grandfather!" None of us made any money, but we were given a parting gift of some low-valued cash. (Fredrick, SS, 4/17).

Upstairs the Stone Soup people were making a special effort to make the visiting Traders (the Sapphire team) feel welcome. They shared their breakfast, inquired politely about the Traders' grandmothers, listened attentively to the Traders' halting responses, and did their best to be gracious hosts. The Fair Trade visitors, however, were intent on playing the Stoner's card game and on winning as much of the Stone Soup money as possible, and so they rushed through these niceties. Once the Stone Soup card games were underway the Stoners gave their money away freely and seemingly at random. While the Traders were ecstatic at this accumulation of wealth, the practice did little to help them understand the subtleties of Stoner Soup culture.

Loretta's Loose Lips

Trader Louise sat down to play the Stone Soup card game with the Sun family of Stoners. Immediately Louise began a friendly but relentless campaign to uncover as much insider knowledge about the Stone Soup culture as she could. Stoner Loretta (a chronically late student who we now know had missed some of the crucial introductory information) happily answered all of Louise's questions (questions that Louise was not supposed to be asking in the first place, and that Loretta was certainly not supposed to be answering at all). Loretta even offered some additional unsolicited information. Nearby Stoners, overhearing snippets of the conversation, tried to interfere, but not before irreparable damage was done. Below are Loretta's profusely apologetic field notes about this event:

Basically I have to write this part first because I have to say first off-I feel soooooooooo bad about what happened in class, I didn't realize what had happened until after class when I got the e-mail sent out to everyone about how we are in grave danger. It made it seem so serious-I knew that I had said a few things that I shouldn't have looking back-but it was due to a "miscommunication." Before the Stone Soup meeting started we were passing the name tags and plastic bags around and I had a bunch of them right where I was sitting so people were asking me for them. I found out later from a group member that it was around that time that Rachel had mentioned that we were sup-posed to interact with the Trading culture members, but I didn't hear the part about not telling them any details about our culture. They did not know how to play our game so I explained the rules to them. I thought I remembered hearing that the treasured ones were not allowed to talk unless we gave them permission, so somewhere in the conversation with one of the Traders I told her who our treasured one is and that she was now allowed to speak with him. She then inquired about why we did this. I replied that they are special to us, and that we protect them. The two girls at the table looked uncomfortable, but looking back that was probably the point, but I made every effort to make them feel welcome. I then asked them about their culture and said that I had heard about money and that it means a lot in their culture, and she proceeded to tell me that in their culture that being rich was something to be greatly desired, and she wanted to know if that was the same for us. I told her that it was considered rude for us to be too into money and that there was no need anyway because there was enough for everyone. She then mentioned that she heard our Stone Soup asking about Grandmothers and wondered what that was about. I didn't see any harm in telling her that when we greet each other we ask how our Grandmother is doing as a sign of respect. She asked if there was anything else important about our grandmothers and I told her no. We just had a great respect for our ancestors. I also told the girls that the face card was used by our culture to show to someone who is not following the rules because they seemed puzzled by it. Looking back on the whole day I now realize that by trying to help sort of "initiate" them into the culture, I actually hindered our own family and Stone Soup. Because I take the class seriously, and because the class environment really felt like a family-the worst thing in the world happened-I actually felt sad as if I had let my family down. . . I am really, really sorry : (. . . . ." (Loretta, SS, 4/17)

Louise, the Fair Trade visitor who drew all of the Stone Soup secrets from Loretta, tells her side of the story.

When we walked in Rachel handed us a plastic bag with gold coins in it and 5 playing cards. We then split up and went to different tables to play the Stoners' culture's game, or trading with them. The table that

I sat at welcomed me and asked me how my grandma was when I first sat down. They were all very friendly and very welcoming to us. They asked us how we liked our vacation so far, which I assumed was just asking us how it was to visit their culture's territory. I noticed that they all were wearing our money as jewelry and obviously didn't value it the way we did. Before we started playing with them I asked them if they would explain how to play and a girl told me that one person would start by flipping over one of their cards and then everyone at the table would flip over their top card as well. People that had the same color card as the person who started they would give us a coin and if we had a different color we would pay them a coin. While we were playing they asked me about the Traders' culture and if we spoke English or not. I told them no we spoke the Traders' language (I was careful not to translate any of the words or give away any of our secret gestures.) and I asked them about their culture as well. They told me that they don't value money at all but they value each other. They said that their grandma's were very important and that the person who wore a red beaded necklace, called the treasured one, was also very important. At the end of trading when we were about to leave I only had one coin but when I asked the table that I was sitting at if I could have some coins they ended up giving me about 16 coins like it was nothing. They also gave me some of our own money back as well. After we left Stoner culture we went back down to our room and told the Traders what we had seen. (Louise, FTC, 4/17)

Deception and Betrayal

Field notes from the witnesses in both cultures told the same story. Virtually all of the "secret" Stone Soup information had been leaked to the Cartel. My first reaction was dismay. The entire simulation was grounded in the premise that each of the cultures would be opaque to the other, and this was no longer the situation. On reading the field notes, I called for an emergency meeting with Mike and Rachel. I was desperate to recuperate the simulation, the research project, and the course. Later that evening I received my first clue that the situation might be even more complicated than it had appeared. It came in the form of an e-mail from one of the members of Sapphire team (who had visited the Stone Soup on this day). Jade wrote,

Dear Mrs. Wilson, You told us in the first week that if we had something private to say in our field notes we should send them to a different e-mail address. I would like for you to keep my notes of this day private. Can you please tell me where to send them? Thank you, Jade

Jade had been at the same table with Trader Louise and Stoner Loretta and had witnessed the drama that had played out between them. She was also with Louise and the other members of the Sapphire team in the stairwell (just after their visit to the Stone Soup, en route between the two camps) when Louise excitedly shared her newly acquired knowledge with her group. As it became clear to them just how extensive the leak had been, the Sapphire group huddled on the landing between floors and cooked up a plan. They reasoned that if they held back parts of the information they had gathered and distorted some of the bits that they did report, the result would be a distinct advantage for their group in all future cross-culture interactions. Jade was writing to me now (and later came to office hours) to confess that she and Stella (the two shyest members of the Sapphire team) had not been brave enough to oppose the others on the stairs, especially since the plan had won immediate approval from the two male members of their group. Instead Jade and Stella had remained silent (and miserable) while Sapphire delivered their doctored account of the visit to the Cartel. The following is from Jade's private notes.

As we headed back to our classroom, we were talking about how easy it was to get so many coins, and then, one of our group members asked, "Wait, should we tell them that they can just ask for coins, or let them think that the only way to get them is to play the card game?" Then, after a brief discussion, another member took it further to say that we should tell them it was a taboo to ask for coins. Because I had the least amount, he pointed at me and said, "Let's say she (Jade) asked for coins, and the Stoners got really offended, and because the rest of us didn't ask, we got rewarded with lots of coins while she didn't get any." After that Louise said that we should not tell about all of the rules about the red necklace people either. And there came the conspiracy within the same culture.

When we came back in the classroom, other members of the Traders' culture asked about our experience. Louise explained some of the rules of the Stoners' game, and she did a great job describing and explaining some of the details of the game, but she did not say anything at all about the treasured ones or about grandmothers. Sam stepped in to briefly mention that it was a taboo to ask for coins directly. However, it wasn't stressed enough, and one of the members of the group that was scheduled to visit the Stoners' group on Thursday said that he would just ask for coins. Louise looked back at us, but didn't say anything. None of us did. I didn't want to lie, so I was mostly quiet for the whole time, except briefly clarifying the rules of the game.

It was very interesting, and also very sad, to see how we depended on the first group's description of the Traders' culture, and how now we censor, as a group, the information and try to manipulate the other groups' behavior to win this competition among our own culture. I saw the possibility of that there can be a difference between real cultural difference and the cultural difference created by the information carrier/interpreter with conflicting intentions. (Jade, FTC, 4/17)

The research team met the following morning. We contemplated devising new games and rules for the Stone Soup, but were afraid this might compromise the sense of ownership in the culture that we had worked so hard to instill in the Stoners. If nothing else, the imposition of new rules at this point would certainly damage the Stone Soup's morale and slow their momentum. After considerable hand wringing, we reminded ourselves that we were here to observe the development of communication processes and relationships among and between the groups. The form these took would certainly be altered if the simulation, as we had imagined it, crumbled before our eyes, but some form of communications and relationships would surely develop nonetheless. We decided to turn the situation over to the students, take a break from the intercultural activities to give them time to regroup, and see what developed.

PART 3

The Justification

A Few Words about Artifacts and Idiocultures

One distinguishing characteristic of the human species is the capacity, and the necessity, to live in a world transformed by the actions of earlier humans. In what Tomasello (1999) refers to as the "ratchet effect," these transformations are accumulated across generations in the form of artifacts. "Artifact" is a word so inclusive that it is difficult to come up with things that do not fit in its definition. The built world around us and all of the material things in it are artifacts, as are ways of thinking and behaving that have been passed on to us by others who have faced similar situations before. Artifacts can be material, like skyscrapers, diapers, pencils and computers. They can also be ideal, like language, math procedures, and religious beliefs. Culture consists of all the material and/or ideal artifacts accumulated over the social group's history, whether that history is of long or short duration. This cultural inheritance is the toolkit we draw from to effect and mediate our interactions with other people and with the world around us (Cole 1996).

Lev Vygotsky referred to artifact mediated action as the "cultural habit of behavior," which enables human beings to begin to regulate themselves "from the outside" (1994). As A. R. Luria (1928, 493) put it, artifacts incorporated into human action not only "radically change his conditions of existence, they even react on him in that they effect a change in him and in his psychic condition." The tools we use to approach a problem prescribe the kinds of thinking and acting we engage in and the kinds of solutions we can achieve.

An easy way to demonstrate this is to imagine we need to solve a problem involving long division. When we attack the problem with a pencil and paper, we follow a set of cognitive and manual procedures that is quite different from those we use when we solve the same problem with an abacus; and both of those differ from the set we employ when we have a calculator handy. Each time a new tool is incorporated into problem solving, qualitative shifts in thinking occur. The very nature of our thought is altered. Users of an abacus conceptualize the division process quite differently than do users of a calculator. This alters the conditions for future learning, thereby shifting the trajectory of the individual's developmental processes. The methods we begin with when we are first introduced to long division will have lasting effects on our understanding of the process and, by extension, on our understanding of those problems involving long division.

Artifacts are constantly being transformed as they are brought into service in pursuit of changing goals. As contexts evolve new information is acquired and new ways of doing things are developed; the resulting new knowledge is incorporated into the design of the new artifacts, which are passed on in their modified forms to immediate others and to future generations. This ongoing transformation leads James Wertsch to label artifacts "carriers of sociocultural patterns of knowledge" (1994, 204).

Artifacts, as they are created by humans with a purpose in mind, include in their design norms of action and cognition. Remember the abacus? Thus the locus of control belongs neither entirely to the user nor to the artifact, but shifts constantly during use; it is the intentions of the user that direct the use of the artifact, just as it is the design of the artifact that directs the actions of the user. The artifact does not necessarily diminish the role nor amplify the abilities of its user; instead it changes the nature of the task (Cole and Griffin 1987).

Bruno Latour (1996) shows that objects not only mediate and articulate social interactions, but they often initiate them. Latour reminds us that human interactions have no beginning and no end. We are born into ongoing conversations that have extensive histories involving generations of our ancestors. These ancient voices penetrate contemporary dialogue in the form of material, procedural, and ideal artifacts. He offers the example of a post office, which he has entered to purchase stamps. Inside, the

counter, the speaking grill, the door, the walls, the desk, and the chair structure prescribe the interactions between Latour and the postal clerk. How
and where he stands in line, how he speaks through the grill and slides
his money through the slot provided, what vocabulary and manners he
uses are behaviors dictated by the physical characteristics of the post office itself.

A lovely example of the power of an artifact to initiate behavior is offered by Vivian Paley (1986) in *Boys and Girls: Superheroes in the Doll Corner.* Paley tells of her efforts to tame a group of exuberant kindergarten boys
whose running was becoming a problem in the classroom. She brought in
a roll of duct tape and created a running track around the inside perimeter
of the room. The children were told that if they wanted to run, they were
free to do so, as long as they remained inside the confines of the track.
Elsewhere in the classroom they should always walk. Within days the track
took possession of several of the children. Paley reports that some of the
boys would start running even before removing their jackets and putting
their lunchboxes away in the morning. Those lines on the carpet were far
too compelling and had to be removed.

Ed Hutchins (1996) encourages us to imagine ecologies of thinking,
where artifact-mediated human cognition interacts with social environments rich in organizing resources. The artifact becomes one of the many
elements brought into coordination as we perform daily life. These mind
ecosystems exist in perpetual flux, which means that the best way to observe the connections between our history and our future, or between cultural structure and human action, is to mindfully participate in artifact-
mediated activities. Our research brought human actors, in the form of
university students, together for just that purpose. They were provided
with a toolkit of carefully selected artifacts, which were chosen to mediate
the students' activities inside a prepared social environment, which itself
existed inside a larger ecology of organizing resources.

Gary Alan Fine (1987) uses the term "idioculture" to describe the cultural formations (the unique collections of material and behavioral artifacts
and relationships among the people and artifacts) that emerge in small
groups. He holds that to understand the persistence and evolution of cultural practices, we must consider what these practices mean to the actors.
An idioculture, or the "meaningful traditions and artifacts of a group; ideas
behaviors, patterns of verbalization, and material objects" (124) emerges

from collective intentional activity and develops and evolves over time in response to the challenges that the group experiences. It is important to clarify that the term "idioculture" does not refer to the individuals who make up a cultural group (although the idioculture can be manifest only through the actions of group members), but to the group's unique cultural package. Fine's work with little league baseball helps to make this clear. A team's players, coaches, and spectators will come and go. The location and specifics of the ballpark may change. The uniforms and equipment all undergo transformation over time. Even the rules of the game are subject to interpretation. But an enduring, cohesive set of ideal forms of the physical and procedural tools of the game, and of ways of thinking and playing, persists and is normalized within a group of players; this, according to Fine, is the idioculture of a little league baseball team (Fine 1979). "Members of a group recognize that they share experiences, and that these experiences can be referred to with the expectation they will be understood by other members, thus being used to construct a reality for the participants" (124).

In research like ours it is useful think of the two different collections of cultural products that develop through the simulation as two different idiocultures, and to think of the enculturation of the students as the appropriation and mastery of those particular artifacts that are key to life inside their own idioculture. In other words, when a person can engage fluidly with others in their group, use the appropriate language and behaviors, effectively employ the local tools, and interpret others' actions using the group's standards and ethics, that person is judged to be a fully enculturated member of the group.

Human behaviors are difficult to interpret. We rarely know what all of the actors are thinking in any social interaction, but we can observe the ways the mediating artifacts are used. When social relations are complex and ambiguous, we can sometimes focus on the artifacts that mediate the interactions, on the ways they are selected, employed and transformed, to gain a better understanding of what is going on.

At this point in the simulation the students had fully appropriated the few simple tools and procedures they had been given and were now reshaping them to meet the challenges they were facing. Keep in mind that the two idiocultures did not appear magically but were created out of cultural "starter kits" that were developed from the already existing cultures inhabited by the researchers. The Stoner and Trader idiocultures were embedded inside the larger culture of the class and, by extension, of the university and its environs. Now, as the pages to follow demonstrate, these idiocultures were expanding and evolving into hybrid cultures displaying influences from the class activities and from the cultural heritages of the people comprising the two groups.

April 22nd: The Stoners Invoke a Hurricane.
The Traders Weather It, Poorly.

The next time the Fair Trade visitors (the Bella trading group) entered Stone Soup territory, there were none of the usual greetings, no home-baked goodies, and no cheerful music playing. Instead of being greeted by a tribe of naïve natives who were unaccountably happy to part with their money, they found the room empty—except for Professor Mike, who was sitting all alone in the corner with his laptop computer. (He regularly dropped in on both cultures, so his presence was not out of the ordinary.) He appeared to be just as baffled as the Traders were. No, he had not seen anyone from the Stone Soup this morning. He pointed out the hand-drawn picture (a tropical island scene) taped to the front door. Professor Mike mused for a few minutes with the Trading group about what the drawing might signify and what might have happened to the Stone Soup. "No clue really, but you guys let me know when you find out," and then he retreated to his office.

The Bella group hung around the empty room for a while, hoping the Stoners would show up. Nothing. Finally, the disappointed Traders ate the oranges that they had brought to share and returned home to find the other members of the Fair Trade just as confused. The trading session had opened as usual. The Traders were ready and waiting for today's Stone Soup visitors and, more importantly, for their exceedingly valuable trading cards. But the expected visitors did not arrive—which meant the Fair Trade profits for the day would be meager at best.

In another building on campus the Stoners were in conclave. *"The day we went to higher ground to escape the hurricane"* (Melissa) was one of introspection for the Stone Soup. Each Stoner had received an e-mail from Rachel the day before that read:

Stone Soup's secrets, rules, traditions, and games have become known to the Outsiders. This has laid bare our culture, our grandmothers, and our heritage, and left us extremely vulnerable. We will need to find ways to protect ourselves. (Rachel, SS, 4/20)

This had been followed by a change of venue notice, telling the Stoners not to approach their old classroom but to show up for class at a new room in a different building on campus. (No special communication of any kind was sent to the Fair Trade Cartel.) In the heated online conversation that had ensued among the Stoners, one of the Stone Soup families decided to create a sign and leave it for the Traders, who they knew would be visiting the old location and expecting to find a greeting party. Jaime wrote, *"Having no written language, we left a drawing showing a hurricane ravaged island and our people traveling to higher ground."* The Stoners were never told that they had no written language. In fact, they kept a "Book of Stone Soup Knowledge" where many of the entries were in English. But their communication with the Fair Trade Cartel had never been written, and on this occasion they all agreed that the sign they left for the visiting Traders should be pictorial.

As soon as the Stoners were assembled in their secret meeting place, everyone in Loretta's family took some heat from the other Stone Soup families about the leak. They had, after all, sat and listened while she spilled all the Stone Soup's secrets. Why had they not intervened? In the end the requisite reprimands were brief and surprisingly kind. It was quickly decided that some of the Stone Soup practices should be changed and made more difficult to decipher. But which ones? To a person, the group insisted that the Stone Soup worldview, with its emphasis on community, hospitality, and kindness, must be maintained.

The remainder of the class period was spent devising new games and new ways of communicating that were true to the Stone Soup's values but were less transparent and could be implemented in time for the next class meeting. Several new card games were introduced, stricter rules governing the "treasured ones" were instated, the Stone Soup's pot of gold coins was "buried," and a new form of coinage took its place.

One of the Stone Soup procedural artifacts that was a part of the original game was the use of special cards to reprimand a player for ignoring the Stone Soup rules. Should a player break one of the Stone Soup rules, the offended party was to stop speaking and hold a censure card up in front of the offender for a few seconds and then turn and walk away. The practice had been suggested in week one of the simulation, but the students had never implemented it. Now the Stoners chose to introduce it, using kings, queens, and jacks to notify other players that they were ignoring important rules. The Stoners hoped this might help them monitor the Traders' behavior as well as add another layer of complexity to their image.

Through all of this adversity the Stone Soup was strangely animated—happy even—in a way that they had not been before. Rachel noted that they appeared to be *"bonding"* and to have become a *"more cohesive group"; "they exude this sense of us, united against the world."* The students' field notes supported her observations. For the first time the Stoners had a concrete problem to solve together, one that they could really sink their collective teeth into. This was far more compelling than any of their earlier tasks that had all been aimed at the rather vague goal of becoming a culture of gentle people. Below is Fredrick's retrospective on the day's events.

> *We found out one of our friends had shared the secrets of our Stone Soup with members of the Traders' culture during their visit. I was not sure what many others felt about the situation, but I know that I was slightly perturbed that such a blatant boundary could be so carelessly crossed. However, being friends and a resourceful people, we were able to meander around any real potential problems. During a "hurricane" that hit our territory, we met in another safe room where we could discuss possible solutions while remaining faithful to the simulation. Some examples of solutions were changing our card game by using the face card as a means of entry (along with its other use as a disciplinary tool) and changing the coinage which we would win in the game with replicas of U.S. coins. Our theory was that the Traders would be confused and wish to know what different values the coins had. Of course, not valuing money, we would simply reply that they were gifts. This was indicative of the key differences between our two cultures. (Fredrick, SS, 10/22)*

Fredrick was not alone. Field notes from the Stoners revealed a uniform and consistent understanding of what the Stone Soup culture was about and what it meant to be a member. Dennis commented on how congruent the many self-descriptive qualities appeared to be, each one resonating with the others; he notes, for example, that the Stone Soup's *"kind-*

ness and lack of focus on money" worked perfectly with its *"ethic of tolerance and generosity."* Fredrick agrees.

> *All the qualities that we would use to describe our culture, all of them, were compatible with one another, for instance unity, sharing, understanding, kindness, love, friendship, and of course our traditions. Everyone engaged the discussion pretty well and all had good ideas. I also think that this got us to act and think more as a group, which could only result in further cooperation and identification with each other. I think this simulation has certainly proven itself to be a very organic and fluid endeavor in a very short time, which itself is exciting. (Fredrick, SS, 4/22)*

The only real problem was that the core qualities defining the Stone Soup culture (e.g., openness and absence of aggression) were the same ones that laid it bare to exploitation. This contradiction was not internal to the Stone Soup but sprang from their interaction with the Cartel, and it proved to be the Catch-22 that stalled many of the Stone Soup's efforts to move forward. Any attempts to defend the Stone Soup lifestyle from outsiders, hiding their money and mystifying their rituals, for example, would alter that very lifestyle and violate the Stone Soup's codes of generosity and openness. During the conclave the group attempted to resolve this on a case-by-case basis, adjusting the rules as possible scenarios came up for discussion. Everyone present agreed that the repeated tweaking of the Stone Soup rules would eventually undermine some of the Stone Soup's most cherished traditions, but no one had a better suggestion. Melani's notes were typical.

> *I knew exactly what the Stoners are supposed to exemplify. We are peaceful, respectful to other cultures, protective of our own members, and we value our members' wellbeing over material objects. I was surprised when we began to share that I had neglected to mention other important aspects and even vital aspects of our culture such as storytelling, card games, ancestry, creativity, affection, and fun. I listened when others shared. Much of what they said was similar to what I thought. I was relieved the Stone Soup was thinking similarly to me. This meeting was distinctly different from the previous simulations. Usually the rules are stated and then the simulation begins. In this meeting however, we as members in the simulation were*

*not only discussing the rules but discussing how the rules could be altered.
I really enjoyed the change of the environment and the participation in
creating new rules, but I think I should have been more proactive for certain
opinions during the meeting. However, at the time I felt that being too argu-
mentative would not have been in accordance to the Stone Soup's ways. The
large importance of these changes to the culture has become clearer after reflection on the meeting. Our problem during the simulation seems to be lack
of understanding how to interact with the Traders without explaining our
rules. This is difficult because we are a very social culture that tells stories.
So I think the confusion lies in determining the line between a story and an
explanation of our ways. (Melani, SS, 4/22)*

The only Stoner ethic that was not negotiable was the importance of
treating others kindly, as Sailer notes: *"We decided that whatever we did we
still needed to keep our commitment about always being kind to others."* The field
notes suggested that they took this commitment most seriously when re-
lating to other Stoners, and that this period of contemplation about Stoner
values resulted in a new sense of unity or camaraderie among the Stone
Soup members. Stoner JuLi shares her understanding of the crisis facing
her group.

All of our answers were similar—kindness, open mindedness, high
integrity, Grandmother and history, touch, happy and fun, treasured
ones, sharing, no secrets from each other, etc. This hurricane definitely
brought us unity. This is the first time where almost everyone contributed to the Stone Soup meeting. However, because we had so many
different ideas, it was rather difficult to decide on what strategy to use
for games, and for vacations. Although we had various different ideas,
and had difficulty deciding on one particular solution to our problem,
we felt stronger than ever. We had a common goal in mind—share our
values, yet protect ourselves from the Traders' culture at the same time.
The hurricane reflected what drama and performance can bring to a
culture, both the positives and the negatives. We felt invaded, unpro-
tected when our secrets leaked out to the Traders, but we didn't simply
sit there, complain, or cry, we transformed our sadness into strength.
Although the hurricane hit us unexpected, we were able to work
through our problems, and solve the difficulties as a group, we were

able to take advantage of both the positives and the negatives of the hurricane drama to change the view of Stone Soup culture, hopefully for the better. (JuLi, SS, 4/22)

Going to the Mattresses

The new camaraderie shared by the Stoners stood in stark contrast to the disharmony brewing in the Fair Trade Cartel where conversations were growing increasingly edgy and accusatory. Field notes on "the day the Stone Soup Tribe went missing" (Harry) show that the two cultures were approaching the breach in totally different ways. No one in the Fair Trade group asked, "Who are we?" or "What core values define us?" Instead, accusations about what specific acts individual Traders may have committed to provoke such a drastic response from the Stone Soup and arguments about what could be done to rectify the situation swelled in volume until a staff member down the hall stepped in and asked us to keep it down.

After the first onslaught of recriminations ("She made a really cool bracelet for you out of $5 bills, but instead of wearing it, you took it apart right in front of her and put it in your money envelope." [Anna]), **personal confessions dominated the conversation** ("I think I was really rude to the girl I was trading with, and I took two cards from her when I really only paid for one." [Jenn]). It was widely assumed that the Fair Trade had offended the Stone Soup with the blatant negative use of the word "grandma" and overly aggressive trading, but there was also an undercurrent of irritation. ("I think it was not right for them to leave without giving us any warning." "They can't just do this to us, can they?" "Are they going to lose points for cutting the class?" [Bruno])

As the Traders struggled to figure out what had taken place and what they needed to do to get past it, much of the conversation centered on the "G-Word," as our singular use of the word "grandma" became known in these discussions.

We realized that we'd trivialized the words "Grandma" and "Grandpa" by using them to call one another out on our errors, but these words are obviously important in their culture and it was probably offensive to hear them used in such a way. (Anna, FTC, 4/15)

My newest thought is that maybe we attacked them. Not physically but emotionally. Maybe us using "Grandma" really hurt them and since they treasure their family so much they felt they couldn't be around us. This would also support our idea that they are "family oriented hippies." (Harry, FTC, 4/15)

We all started to throw out different ideas and came to the conclusion that we offended them in some way. . . . We believe they thought we were making fun of them when we called out "grandma, grandma" when someone performed an illegal gesture. The Stone Soup culture values their grandmas very deeply and when we started yelling out "grandma, grandma" they thought we were disrespecting them and their family members. We needed to solve this problem right away in hopes that they would come back. So instead of yelling out "grandma, grandma" when one performs an illegal action, we will call out a number that shows someone did something wrong. For example, if someone shakes their head to say no, instead of using our hand signals, then the person interacting with the offender would yell out, say, "23" and then they would take a card from them as a punishment. (Travis, FTC, 4/15)

Looking in from the Outside

For the most part this story has been told from those of us so deeply embedded in the simulation that impartial judgments are impossible. We were like a bunch of clams trying to describe the chowder. But the notes below are from Bernard, an undergraduate who was observing the Fair Trade discussion on this day. Bernard was not affiliated with either of the cultures as he had missed the first two weeks of class due to illness. Having arrived too late to take part in either of the cultures, we enlisted Bernard as an "unbiased observer," moving between the two groups, making observations and writing field notes from an outsider's perspective.

There was not very much interaction between me and members of the Fair Trade culture. I do not know what caused them to disregard me, it might have been that I had no money, no cards, and could not speak their language. The team that was supposed to vacation in Stone Soup country came back much earlier than expected. They found a 8" × 11.5" picture with mountains and trees in the background, and people in canoes coming up to shore. They assumed that the Stone Soup had left their own country to go to another. They tried to figure out what events might have led the Stoner family to leave their country when they knew visitors were going to be showing up. A couple of people (Traders) pointed out that the Stone Soup family probably thought the Traders were rude.

So what did they decide makes Fair Trade culture rude? They do not really welcome the Stone Soup families when they come in to visit. They give the members of the Stoner family cards to trade, but because of language barriers, the Traders usually exploit this and take their cards. Because time is money, Fair Trade members cannot sit around and chat, or else they are losing money, and that means everything to them. Another key point that they thought about was their mockery of the word "grandma." The Fair Trade clan's language is phonetic, so "grandma" does sound like they are actually saying a word in their language. But since the Traders have turned the word "grandma" into a negative word, and Stoners love talking about their grandmas, this conflict of meaning has created some tension between the two cultures.

One Trader, being frustrated coming back from a disappointing vacation cried, "Let's go to war!" Another said to build a better relationship with them so that they can keep receiving gifts from them. At this time, a part of me wanted to say, "Are you guys really going to do this from the bottom of your heart?" and the other side said, "Are you doing this to gain more material wealth?" I feel like their effort will tip the scale to see where this one goes. It was also interesting to hear comments on adapting some new language and even practices into their culture. They thought that the "welcoming" part should be most important because it sets the tone. It is not in the Fair Trade culture to show warmth and affection, but in order to keep this relationship strong, they are willing to throw in a couple of hugs to welcome the visitors next time around.

In a Darwinian way, I see the Fair Trade culture evolving. They went from trying to maximize their profits, either by exploiting the Stone Soup members when they visited Fair Trade country, or by asking for as much money as possible when they went abroad. But now they are thinking more in terms of optimizing their cash flow, taking more time than usual to greet them during the welcoming, and by not hoarding as much money when they

go abroad so that they do not seem selfish. They are adjusting to fulfill their
needs. (Bernard, outside observer, 4/22)

Both of the cultures were evolving, not only in a Darwinian way as
Bernard suggested, but in a more deliberate Lamarkian fashion as well.
Owing to the structure of the class, the two cultures were obliged to adapt
in concert with one another. Because the simulation was part of university
class, going their separate ways was not an option, and neither group suggested it. The Stone Soup chose to move forward as a more unified, self-
conscious, and cautious group. Although it appeared that the Fair Trade
Cartel would try to rein in some of their ambition to maintain civil trading
relations with the Stone Soup, the group was far from reaching an agreement about this. Some Traders were calling for war.

Despite all of their soul-searching and decisions made to control behaviors believed to have alienated the Stoners, the Traders found these
habits hard to break, particularly the use of the G-word. Its use persisted
and, if anything, proliferated, both inside and outside of class, as Jessica
reports.

> The word "grandma" became so significant to me. We had a debate
> on using the term, and we had a fun time using it. I even started using
> it outside of class. A few days ago, I was in the bookstore and saw a
> book that had the word "grandma" bolded in big font on the cover page.
> I just started giggling because I just naturally thought "someone broke
> the rule." I could imagine shouting "grandma" when I saw that cover
> page. My friend did not understand why I was giggling and even after
> I explained the reason, she did not find it fun at all. (Jessica, FTC, 4/29)

Several student field notes told of instances where the term had been
used spontaneously outside of class, to the confusion of their friends.
Robin shares the following "embarrassing" incident, confirming just how
entrenched the habit had become among the Traders.

> I can't believe the way I think about this class all the time and the way
> some of the fake culture has become so real to me. It can get so embar-
> rassing at times. Last night I was sitting in the Price Center with some of
> my friends and one of them kept stealing french fries from me. Normally

I don't care, but I was really hungry and I told him to go buy his own but he kept stealing mine. When he ate my last one I yelled at him, "You are such a grandma!" Everyone started to laugh at me and I tried to explain about the class but I knew that there was no way they would understand. (Robin, FTC, 4/24)

Alfred Anderson's (1975) research had shown successful groups to be more coherent than those whose efforts are thwarted, so I half expected to see relationships inside the Stone Soup to erode under a barrage of accusations and blame and to see the Traders unite in their victory, but the opposite seemed to be happening here.

The cultures in our simulation did conform, however, to the pattern established by Muzafer Sherif's in the Robbers Cave experiment. Sherif et al. ([1954] 1988) reported that the group who appeared to have the upper hand in any given competition was more apt to loot or deface the other camp's property and more apt to engage in slurs and insults against the "losing" boys. Our simulation was not designed to result in a winning or losing culture, but at this point there did seem to be some perception among the players that the Cartel had assumed a measure of dominance and a threatening attitude toward Stone Soup. (In contrast, the perception within the research team at this time was that the Stoners were in charge. They were acting deliberately, where the Traders appeared to be scrambling, rather frantically, to respond to the changes that the Stoners were instigating.)

As Sherif might have predicted, the Traders were expressing more open mockery and derision toward the Stoners than the Stoners were toward them. Lazy, stupid, childish, and boring were the Traders' most liberally applied adjectives when discussing the Stoners. The research team was both curious and worried about the impact this might have on the developing relationships within and among the two cultures.

In retrospect, the breach in the simulation proved to be a blessing in at least three ways. First, the two groups, under duress, rallied their forces, renegotiated internal alliances, and reinforced in-group/out-group boundaries—all in a very visible way that greatly enriched the research project. Second, the event provoked the groups to invent new practices, untethering the simulation from the original BaFa' BaFa' game procedures, providing numerous examples of the emergence and evolution of artifacts, and allowing for more natural, or less prescribed interactions, both inside and between the two cultures. Finally, in the regrouping period that followed the leak, the students in both groups (the Stoners more than the Traders) spontaneously entered into a sort of "metacultural" phase—an interlude where they explicitly addressed questions about what it meant to be a part of their cultural group, what it might be like to be a part of the other culture, and how the other culture might be perceiving them. At the time, however, these benefits were obscured by other concerns, as Rachel, Mike, and I held our collective breath, not knowing what surprises the next encounter might hold.

April 24th: Reconciliation, or Round Two?

We were hyperaware of the sometimes extreme differences in how participants perceived and interpreted various events of the simulation. Often a dozen or more students and researchers would report on the same event. Without exception, each report introduced new bits of information, and rarely did all of the pieces fit together perfectly. We accounted for these differences by considering the participants' varying frames of reference. Narrative framing is a concept used by both Wertsch (1998, 2002) and Bruner (1991) to talk about the social organization and mediation of perception. Narrative frames are social constructions that impose order on the world by establishing particular attitudes or perspectives, which privilege certain interpretations and preclude others. Conceptual frames of reference often obscure some parts of a scene while making other parts pop into consciousness. These frames come to us from all corners of life and are internalized and reinforced through daily use. Different orders of narrative frames are evident; some are dominant and are constructed over long periods of time through institutions like church, school, or political ideology. Smaller frames are constructed through families, small groups, and personal experience, and may be enduring or fleeting in duration. Often larger frames provide backdrops against which smaller frames are referenced. During this period of reorganization, we watched as the students appeared to be pulling ethical frames from different levels of social context, trying them out, reframing certain events several times, discarding one frame after another until they found one or revised one that made their activities seem meaningful or their actions more palatable.

On the first day back after the breach in procedures, the Stoners arrived with renewed spirit. They had spent the interim days scheming and planning and were now ready to face the Fair Trade Cartel as a more cohesive and prepared collective. This is not to say they were without apprehension, as Fredrick's notes indicate.

> *What really mystified me, though, was how uncomfortable my family and I felt at the prospect of meeting the other culture again, as well as how much we seemed to band together in a sort of defense mechanism. This was also a climactic event to me because it seemed to reveal how much of a group identity we had established over a short period of time. In fact, about five or six Stoners were in the same class directly after our Stone Soup meeting. I had never previously had any desire to walk to class with anyone else at all, but we found ourselves talking and laughing on the way to the next class. This was an interesting phenomena of group dynamics to me, especially in a community where my peers normally separate themselves with iPods and cell phones. (Fredrick, SS, 4/24)*

In contrast, the Cartel appeared fractured and consumed by infighting. Many of them wanted to find ways to appease the foreigners (if the Stone Soup showed up, that is—no one was sure). But others, mainly those who had lost out on trading opportunities, felt the need to be even more aggressive and redouble their efforts to earn as much money as possible in the days that remained.

The Stone Soup did show up and the trading happened, but the students were unsettled and the interactions were awkward and out of sync. The demeanors of both groups showed distinct shifts. The Stoners were wary and protective. Traders were tentative and seemed to be handling the Stoners with kid gloves.

At the end of the day Mikelle, one of the Cartel's more successful traders, laughingly admitted that for the first time she had actually slowed down enough to look the visiting Stoners in the face. She said she had never even thought of them as people before, but as carriers of the cards she needed to complete her sets. Her field notes, which follow, reveal some frustration on her part, but also some effort to understand the actions of the Stoners she was trading with, a first for Mikelle.

I noticed that trading with the Stoners today was more difficult than before. I think it's because the group today was actively trying to figure out the game and thought they had an idea of how the game works. This made it difficult for me because they would offer me other cards even though I could see the card I needed in their hand. If I asked again for it, they would motion "no" and get me to go away. If I waited and asked again they would still say no because they thought they didn't have it. The visitors that came today were looking at the bolts on the cards. This was very interesting to me because I had never noticed that different cards had different amount of bolts on them before. For example I was asking for a yellow 3 and one of the Stoners told the other "she's looking for a card with 5 bolts." In the past they just tried to do whatever we wanted them to do, but now they were very determined and were looking at the cards in a completely different way and therefore there was no way we could communicate with each other. It was difficult and frustrating to trade with them. I'm not sure if they thought they knew what I wanted, although they had no clue and I couldn't tell them in English, or if they were deliberately trying to play dumb to try and get more information from me. After today's meeting I think that the thing that is standing in our way to excel as a culture isn't only the language anymore but the way we trade with the Stoners. We haven't been able to find a common ground where we understand each other. I think this isn't happening because we are all afraid that they will figure out our game and trade within themselves to drain our bank. We can't let them know the game, but if we don't, it makes it harder for us to get what we want from them. (Mikelle, FTC, 4/24)

Jaime from Stone Soup writes about the same event. Her notes provide a sense of the Stoners' experience on this day and show that the Traders had indeed softened their approach, but that the Stoners were not as naïve or trusting as they had been in the past.

Today the hurricane had passed. As we took our quizzes, a piece of paper circulated around the classroom. It said "We missed you Stoners" or something to this effect. I thought it was a joke because this crayon illustration showed people holding hands. My group exited feeling a bit leery. Were the

Traders going to receive us harshly "yelling grandpa" and abrasively play the game with us? Or were they going to show more consideration after our hurricane dislocation? My family traveled to the foreign land of the Traders. We entered into the room and our presence wasn't at all felt. I even said "We're here!" and no one really looked up. One person noticed, but then resumed to their exchange. We looked at the swapping of various cards and colors. It seemed all very foreign, the chanting of random terms that I knew nothing of their significance.

In order to fully immerse ourselves in the Traders' culture, the Maple family wanted to play this game. No one invited us into this game, but we remembered that Deborah served as the cashier. We went up to her, and gave her our copper and silver coinage. Deborah seemed delighted but perplexed all at once. She took our gift, and gave us stacks of cards individually. In order to have an even amount of each color, all five of us traded amongst ourselves to have evenness of the green, orange, yellow, white, and orange colored cards. We tried to protect our "treasured" one and our "treasured" ones keeper made sure she was safe. With this, I felt a freedom to explore and engage the Traders. This time the Traders actually spoke English. I said "hello" expecting nothing in return, and I surprised to be met with a "hi." I pushed my luck further, asking about his grandmother, and he responded with that his grandmother is doing great. We dived into the game. He made a signal saying a certain word I didn't understand. After a few interactions, I began to realize that "wa" meant white, "ra" meant red, "ga" meant green, and so forth. The words after the color identification probably signal the number of bolts or apples on the card. This Trader tried to have me understand the card he was asking about. He pointed to one of my red cards that had one bolt as he signaled an exchange for one of his green cards with one bolt. I had made a successful exchange! This was the only exchange I was able to make for the whole visit.

I continued to be caught off guard by their friendliness. They genuinely attempted to help me in my comprehension of the game. I didn't quite understand the premise of the exchange because a card that matched the bolts on another color card didn't make for a successful exchange. They waved their arms at their sides, and then left. No one chanted "grandpa" or seemed hostile towards me when I inquired about their grandmother. This was a relief! However, one Trader seemed very intent on his trading. He got really into the game, and he deeply sighed when a match could not be made. I guessed he

*was probably really close to winning or something of the sort. After learning
a bit more about the game, the Maple family looked at the desks where the
Traders stored their possessions. Envelopes marked with the writing "Bella
trading co" and "Sapphire investment group" were on different tables. This
led all of us to gather that the game was a trading game. The cards did not
probably have a universal value but the value was subjective to a specific
company. Here no kinship and family units broke up their table groups, but
rather the association of money-making aims.*

*Deborah rang the bell for all of us to finish trading. We went up to her,
and I gave her a handful of green cards. The last group said that these were
worth the most. She told me no exchange could be made. I tried again gathering cards from my fellow Maples. I put together five white cards all with
one bolt, but again Deborah could not make a trade. I have yet to discover
what this means. Although I feel closer to deciphering their language, there
is still so much mystery that serves as a barrier between the Stoners and
Traders. However, this distance is becoming less overwhelming. We said
goodbye to the Traders, and all of them wished us a friendly farewell. They
were courteous and sociable! What a drastic transformation! (Jaime, SS,
4/24)*

The traveling Traders arrived in Stone Soup territory to a slightly
cooler reception than their colleagues had enjoyed in weeks past. Each
Stoner family seemed to be playing a different card game, and the hosts
were far less forthcoming with advice and information about how to play.
The Traders also noticed that the large gold doubloons that had been so
carelessly strewn around the room had been replaced with much less im-
pressive silver ones. None of this slowed the Traders down. The Stoners
were both amused and disgusted as they watched the "thieving Traders"
(Jeff) scooping up with abandon the worthless coins that stood in for the
now buried clan treasure.

*I don't think the girls from the other culture got the point of the game—but
they have caught on that money is not of huge significance to us. When it
was time to leave us, the two girls decided on their own without asking that
it was okay to take most of the coins in our pile. They thought that it was
just as valuable as the gold coins, and that in the end—they could exchange
these coins for something valuable. I thought it was rude and impolite that*

they did not ask if it was okay to take our coins, but since our culture does not value wealth in terms of cash and coins, it should not matter, right? Either way, it is still impolite! Sorry, but I think they are thieving traders! I feel like their culture is a "dog-eat-dog" world, and reaching to the top of the ladder in society may mean that you need to step over some boundaries. If only their society wasn't so focused on material wealth! That is why I like our culture a lot more—because wealth is not measured in terms of monetary value, but of how deeply connected we are to our grandmothers (which is our history, our foundation) and to each other. There is no hatred, but lots of happiness and laughter. (Mandy, SS, 4/24)

As relationships between the Stone Soup and Fair Trade cultures were being renegotiated, relationships within the groups were shifting as well. One dramatic example was the transformation we observed in the trading interactions that involved some of the Asian women in the Fair Trade Cartel. Early in the simulation Jade, who is Korean, told me there was never a moment in the simulation when she was not aware of her "Korean-ness," a sentiment that was echoed by several other Korean women in the class. In the first week we assured all of the students that they were not compelled to do anything in the simulation that felt wrong to them; they could simply say "no" without penalty. I asked that, if they felt comfortable doing so, they include sections in their field notes explaining the logic or sentiments behind a decision not to participate. Jade chose to take part in all of the activities and then wrote detailed and thoughtful notes about her struggle to reconcile the requirements of the class with her cultural habits. She begins one of her field notes with the following.

I was born and raised in South Korea, where people value social harmony and being considerate and thoughtful in understanding each other's needs and wants even without words, more than being aggressive, direct and fast in getting what you want. I felt from the beginning that the Fair Trade culture was conflicting with my native culture. This simulation has been a genuine cultural struggle of my own. (Jade, FTC, 4/22)

After reading Jade's notes I called her in to office hours to be sure that she was holding up and not feeling pressured into doing anything that ran contrary to her beliefs. She assured me that she was fine, and her next set of field notes contained this affirmation.

> In this class I'm doing things I have never done before. I never really pushed myself to try the ways of American girls, although sometimes I would wish I could. Now I know what it feels like to be more aggressive and sometimes even loud. I don't think this will ever be the way I am, but I am happy to say that I have tried it. (Jade, FTC, 4/24)

Stella was struggling with many of the same issues. Early in the simulation she "felt sad" because she knew that her (male) teammates were frustrated with her tentative participation in the trading sessions. "They tried to be nice but they kept saying that each one of us should work to add to the Sapphire money totals and then they would look at me to make sure that I understood. I did understand but it was hard for me to speak out in an American way."

In the first few days of the simulation Stella and Jade spent a lot of time trading with each other, which was more comfortable for them but did little to increase their wealth or their perceived value to their trading houses. In Jade's comments below, we see that she is rethinking her earlier interactions with Stella, not knowing whether to attribute Stella's kindness to team affiliation, friendship, or their shared Korean backgrounds.

> During my very first trade with one of my group members, Stella, she offered to give me the card I needed for whatever card I didn't need in exchange, even though she knew that I didn't have any card she really needed. For the first time I felt some kind of group mentality. Then I assumed that it was because we seemed to share the same value of serving others and avoiding unnecessary competitions for the sake of social harmony, but now I wonder. Did I assume we were thinking the same because she gave me what I needed, because we were on the same team, or because she just looked like me because she is Korean like me. (Jade, FTC, 4/24)

Both Jade and Stella voiced the opinion that the rigid gender roles they were accustomed to meant that the simulation was a lot easier on the Korean males in the class than it was on them, but they were resourceful women and discovered a loophole. The cultural pressure they felt for high scholastic performance was not gender specific. The imperative to do well in the class far outweighed the requirement to maintain a demur demeanor. Following this logic, they were able to overcome any discomfort they might be feeling at pushing the boundaries of polite behavior. The women's eventual willingness to step outside their comfort zones and fully participate in the decidedly impolite trading was remarkable. I had been prepared to give them considerable leeway in their participation grade, but in the end there was no need for that. Not only did they jump in and take part in the trading, but they became formidable competitors.

An unexpected effect of the game was that once Jade and Stella gave themselves permission to fully participate in the aggressive trading, their insider's position in the trading culture provided them with an outsider's perspective on their own South Korean heritage, as Jade reports below.

> Because the Fair Trade Culture is very different than my own native culture, first I felt a strong resistance to accept the trading rules, and my conflicts of value system had begun. At the same time as I "naturally" resisted to absorb the Fair Trade's cultural values because of my native culture, I was rationally preoccupied by following the Fair Trade values of making trade efficiently and making maximum profits. I felt pressured to do well in trading as I assumed it would be reflected in my class grade, since my native culture valued education highly. In this process, I became uncomfortable with my own values and began the re-evaluation process of my own culture. Some of the parts were not compatible with the others. I was expected to be quiet and polite, but I was also expected to do whatever was necessary to be successful in school. (Jade, FTC, 4/24)

In class Bruno, who is also Korean, was the consummate shark—just ask him. He was the self-appointed leader of his trading team, avid defender of the most aggressive Fair Trade practices, and outspoken basher of all things associated with the Stone Soup culture. He wrote long and impassioned field notes defending his positions on everything from trading policies to donut selections. From his brash behavior in class I had imagined Bruno to be oblivious to the concerns of Jade and Stella, so I was more than a little surprised to find the next passage among his notes.

I'm thinking that the transition from Korean to American culture is much harder for females than it is for males. I have to say honestly that I don't have any problem exploiting the Stoners, or even the other trading groups, if it means I can earn more cash. I do feel differently about the Bella group though. I want them all to win something. Just not as much as me. I think Korean businessmen are just as aggressive as Americans and they are probably more corrupt. There are also Korean "Dragon Ladies" in business as well, but I guess no little girl really wants to grow up and be one. I don't know though, maybe they do. (Bruno, FTC, 4/24)

One More Day

Since the first trading day following the hurricane, when the Traders had voted to allow the Bella group a second opportunity to travel to Stoner territory to make up the day they had lost, the Country Inc. trading team had been lobbying incessantly for an additional trading day as well. Country Inc. had been the first group to travel into Stone Soup territory, but this had been an observational mission in which they were not permitted to interact with the locals. The team was angry because they were the only ones having had no opportunity to trade in foreign currency, a circumstance that put them seriously behind in earnings. Country Inc. put their case to the rest of the Cartel, who understood their plight and, in the spirit of Fair Trade, decided unanimously that we should carry on for one more day.

April 29th: A Bit of Moral Reckoning
(and an Intercultural Marriage)

On day nine, when the cultures exchanged visitors for the last time, the Stoners were visibly more relaxed than they had been since the hurricane, and the Traders were again wearing their "trade-with-me" smiley faces. In Fair Trade territory it was business as usual. The Stoners still struggled to figure out the Traders' language and the rules of trade, while the Traders rushed to take full advantage of this last opportunity to relieve the Stoners of their most valuable playing cards, but the general mood was uncharacteristically light-hearted and congenial. Upstairs in Stone Soup country the atmosphere was downright festive, and in one corner of the room a mixed-culture marriage ceremony was underway! In this impromptu wedding all of the complexities that had developed in the Fair Trade/Stone Soup makeshift exchange system bubbled to the surface.

The wedding appeared benign enough, almost trivial, as it was taking place. Dennis, the groom, did not even mention it in his field notes. But the story of the occasion took on new importance with each retelling by the other students, and its subsequent interpretations by members of both cultures were curious and complex. As Robin, the bride, told the story to her fellow Traders (but not in her own field notes), she approached one of the male members of the Stone Soup (nameless to her at this point) who was wearing a "feathered" headband that he had fashioned from Fair Trade money. She complimented him on his work and asked whether he would make one for her as well . . . but out of fifties instead of ones. He readily agreed, fashioned an almost-matching headband for her, and proudly placed it on her head. Someone produced a camera and snapped the couple's photograph. This pleased Robin, who began to pose and tell the group that she and ("What is your name, anyway? Dennis? Hi, Dennis!") Dennis had just been pronounced husband and wife. Those in the immediate vicinity all give similar, and equally insignificant, accounts of the episode, but as the story made its way through the class it took on disapproving overtones, as these increasingly uncomplimentary comments demonstrate.

> I heard laughter from the table behind us and saw that Robin was being crowned with a sort of headdress made of money attached to a string. The guy putting it on her head wore one just like it. I exclaimed, "You guys are married now!" and pulled out my cell phone to take pictures. I took a picture of the "bride," a picture of the crowning, and a picture of the "newlyweds." Fifteen minutes were up and it was time to go. Our group invited us to take our winnings and our new fans and jewelry. We gladly accepted (and helped ourselves to some more coins as well) and went back downstairs to the Cartel. We told the rest of the Cartel about the willingness of the Stoners to give us money, which is an experience that everyone else who visited them can identify with. We talked about the engagement and the wedding, and everyone had a good laugh. (Ally, Robin's teammate, FTC, 4/29)

Apparently, one of the girls got married into the other colony, which was a whole new ritual that we were unfamiliar with. She came back with a crown and she seemed really upbeat about being married so I assumed the ceremony was really cheerful, etc. The main thing I really focused on from their account is that they said they were able to get lots of money and even asked for the jewelry cash, which was technically mutilated tender. A member of her group even stated something along the lines of they didn't care if it was destroyed, it was still money. This is interesting in that I probably would have thought the same way, but in perspective, they were having this beautiful wedding ceremony, but her group was still focusing on getting money and winning in our culture. It seems that the 2x a week ritual of our culture has really gotten a hold on our mental state. It could be the promise of a reward at the end or just getting caught up in the game but it really does seem to be affecting us. I am curious if the other culture are as into the game and their cultural (probably family/social values rather than monetary gain) as we are. (Sam, FTC, 4/29)

I was extremely surprised to learn that the Cartel members joined us in making origami out of their money because they were trying to smuggle back some of the money! When the girls came to visit our family, I really believed they were making origami because they liked the jewelry and wanted to make some for themselves and to take back to their family members. I thought they were different outside their culture, but they proved me wrong. They even went so far as to have a wedding ceremony so that they could make a money headdress, but then they took it back and took it all apart for the cash. They have carried their greedy cultural beliefs with them on to vacation. (Dennis's family member, Jasmine, SS, 4/29)

Although the bride is quoted discussing the wedding in several other participants' field notes, in her own she mentions neither Dennis nor the ceremony—focusing instead on the Stoners' money-based handicrafts.

By this time I had paid very little attention to the game that was going on, and was more concerned with participating in their culture. I watched all the Stone Soup members create beautiful objects out of the money they had; one made a frog, another made an origami turtle,

and another made a bracelet. When leaving the Stone Soup culture and
heading back down to the Cartel culture, all my group members were
referencing to how much money was on my head, they did not care
how or where I got it but were more concerned to how much money it
was. They were saying things like, "Oh my God Robin you have so much
money on your head." I really did not care about the money because
if I did I would have immediately taken it off my head to count how
much was there, but instead I was trying to understand the way of their
culture. (Robin, FTC, 4/29)

The field notes from this day were some of the most extensive of the
simulation. Now accustomed to writing every night about the challenges
that had emerged during the day's activities, and having experienced little
that day that was contentious, the students took the opportunity to muse
about the moral dilemmas they were grappling with in the simulation.

The majority of the Stone Soup members reported feeling like they
had developed close bonds with the others in their culture, and they attributed this closeness to the Stone Soup mandate to put relationships first
and to the Stone Soup activities that provided opportunities to build those
relationships. They were still struggling with the feeling they were unable
to protect themselves from exploitation by the Fair Trade Cartel. The old
dilemma persisted; the things that the Stoners cherished most about their
culture—being open, friendly, and noncompetitive—were the very qualities that left them vulnerable to the Traders' aggressive tactics. Ongoing
discussions about how to proceed always produced what Stoner Mandy
called *"a depressed recognition that the culture our group has so carefully culti-
vated is doomed."* Mandy adds:

> It doesn't help that we really have no way to disagree with each other about
> what should be done to protect ourselves. No matter what anyone says,
> our culture demands that we listen politely and be supportive. That's nice,
> but sometimes it just doesn't get us anywhere. We don't seem to be able to
> make any difficult group decisions. (Mandy, SS, 4/29)

Several Stoners mentioned a *"silver lining"* (Sailer) that accompanied
their exploitation by the Traders, a new sense of unity and pride among
Stone Soup members. The day taken off for regrouping was cited as a turn-

ing point in Stone Soup solidarity. I particularly like Melani's comments, which follow; she describes the Stone Soup's *"loving yet suspicious"* stance toward the Fair Trade culture.

> We had been through a lot of hard times together and now the classroom atmosphere was mostly comfortable throughout the simulation. Most of the activities seemed to flow into each other rather smoothly. There was no awkwardness or nervousness between conversations. By now our culture as a whole seemed to be a collective group rather than a bunch of individual students placed within a classroom. If there were moments of quiet or silence it was not out of not being comfortable within the group but probably general fatigue or simply just busy with a task at hand.
>
> I thought it was funny that we had this loving and yet suspicious attitude toward the other culture, and yet it felt to me at the time to be a fairly justified suspicion. I thought the foreigners were to us like our little siblings; we love them but sometimes they don't always act appropriately and need to be monitored. I always felt slightly exhausted after visiting them, and good to be back in my own culture where I knew that I would be welcomed and treated with kindness and respect. I think they noticed it too, because they seemed like different people outside their room. When they came to visit us they were really very nice. We really owe the other culture in some ways. Without them we would not know ourselves so well, because we would not have taken the time to stop and think about what was important to us and what wasn't, about what things we wanted to keep and what we could change in order to make ourselves less transparent. (Melani, SS, 4/29)

In her midterm reflection Jaime tells us that, as a group, the foreigners were intimidating and strange, but as she got to know them individually, she discovered common ground and became more comfortable in their company. Below she discusses her efforts to define her own culture through getting better acquainted with the Other.

> While hearing about the way of the Cartel (while maintaining our friendly and unaffected attitude towards money) I contemplated the humor of having an opposite culture completely contradictory to our social codes. This irony became a lived reality as we encountered a people who squirmed at the thought of being asked about their grandmother. They treated us as children

*in such a condescending fashion, and my own UCSD mentality wanted to
fight back. A struggle to hold true to the Stoners' peacefulness proved almost
too much for me in the beginning. Witnessing their desperation to win our
games and even steal our money, my anger eventually turned to pangs of
sympathy as I began to realize how much I appreciated my own culture. The
exposure to the Cartel strengthened my own idea of what it meant to be a
part of the Stone Soup Culture. (Jaime, SS, midterm)*

Meanwhile the Traders were grappling with very different issues. The
Stoners had used the earlier retreat as a period of introspection, but the
Traders had not. Only now did the Fair Trade Cartel members begin to
take a closer look at their own motivations. Where they had previously
given straightforward one-sided overviews of their encounters with the
foreigners, they were now delving deeper, trying to unpack their own actions and rationales as well as those of the other players. Hisako, who until
this point in the simulation had written only the briefest and most super-
ficial field notes, begins this day's account by trying to understand what
motivated her teammates to avoid the doughnuts. She then continues to
scrutinize the rest of the morning's events at that same level of detail.

Today, people did not eat many doughnuts. I love doughnuts, and
wanted to eat more, but I hesitated to be greedy, especially because
many people did not touch the doughnuts. I was wondering if the
classmates really did not want to eat doughnuts, or they just pretended
and tried not to be greedy, like me. My stereotyped-American-people[9]
like to eat, and they eat if they want to eat. Also they do not care about
others or what others think, not like Asian people do, so if they want to
eat, they eat as much as they want. There should not be much hesi-
tation in their mind. I know not all Americans are like this and I do
not mean to mention this is good or bad, but it is true that one of the
American cultural attribute is individualism. . . . Thinking about this
for a several minutes, I was surprised how I have stereotyped people
in this way. This is bad. But I am still confused. Were they not hungry?
Were they pretending? I could not find a good reason for why many
doughnuts were left. Why was it? During today's trading, I attempted
to interact with as many as Stone Soup cultural members as possible,

because from the last week's experience, I knew they have so many valuable cards and it is easier to get the card I want from them than from other Cartel cultural members. Since Stone Soup culture do not understand our trading system and do not care about money as much as we do, they are good trading "partners" for us. We were almost exploiting them, without feeling guilty.

I found one Stone Soup girl hiding behind the other Stoner's girl's back, so I tried to talk to her. Surprisingly, she just showed this weird Joker card—she brought it from her class!—and went away from me without saying anything. I lost my words and stood there for a couple of seconds with a shock. I was surprise of her attitude; besides, even for a short second while I stood there, I felt uncomfortable and little bit angry. In our perspective, Stone Soup culture is friendly, talkative, and happy. They are "supposed' to be like that. I might already have stereotyped them; I was angry because they did not act as I expected, and I thought I was disrespected. Since I knew this whole thing was just a simulation game, and I knew exactly why she did that, I mean, I do not understand the purpose but I knew what she has done is based on some Stone Soup cultural rules, I was not really angry. And then I wonder, "If I did not understand her attitude, do I try to understand her? If I cannot understand her, how do I feel about it?" Although I knew about the game, I did get a shock. I laughed after that, because I realized there should be some kind of reasonable meaning in her behavior. But if I believed my stereotype, and judged from my perspective, would I be able to laugh at my situation and her attitude? I don't think so. In the reality, especially as a foreigner in the United States, I often feel disregarded.

Today was the last trading day, so most people kept trading even after the bell was rang. It was very interesting that people are so into this trading game. We are not children, but we still play like them . . . or do we just hate to lose? Finally we went back to the group table and started to arrange their cards. We were not only calculating money but also doing something else . . . we were measuring ourselves according to our culture's rules.

As I was arranging and trying to find the card I needed, I saw Stella was just sitting on her chair, Jeff was counting his money, Harry was collecting all the cards, and Jessica was asking for the card. Each character became so obvious, and I realized that we were constructing small society in the each group. The atmosphere in our group is totally different from other groups; especially, we act like as if we have the roles. We were not given the roles like in the Stone Soup culture, but we were making them by ourselves. I was surprised about the fact, and I was surprised of not realizing of this situation until today, the last day of the trading.

It is hard to judge right or wrong. I sometimes feel there is no right or wrong in the global ideology. You might say I should not be disregarded by some "American attitudes," but how can you tell the person did that attitude on purpose, or without conscious? It is difficult. Even though he or she has not consciously done that attitude, "not knowing what he does" is also bad. I mean, we hurt someone without notice, but the fact we hurt the person remains. So, what should we do? At the beginning, I said I like interacting with people because I do not feel lonely. But interacting with people also makes me lonely. We never overcome our own borders or barriers that we all have, because I am me, you are you; we each are just an individual. I might wander away from the subject, a discussion about the cultural simulation. But I wonder, not being able to understand yourself well, how can I understand others, and others from different culture? (Hisako, FTC, 4/29)

Like Hisako, Sam found it important to factor his Asian heritage into his understanding of his simulation experiences. Sam was particularly interested in drawing connections between what he called the "Confucian family values" that he felt he had been steeped in and the ways he was able to function in the simulation. He shared his belief that many Koreans find it impossible to separate family and business the way that Americans seem to do. Sam's family did business within a system of chaebols, which Sam explains are "large business firms that are privately owned and managed by the founders and their families. Within Korean chaebols, outside recruitment is non-existent and ownership is restricted to blood relations." Americans, Sam writes, are often torn between their commitments to their jobs and their families, and so each of those priorities is weakened by the other. For Koreans, responsibilities to family and employer are often one and the same and therefore undivided and intensified. In all cases, family and chaebol come first. Individual needs, when considered at all, take a very distant back seat. This arrangement conflicted head on with the Fair Trade Cartel system where individual accomplishment was paramount, trading teams a distant second, and loyalties to the Cartel came into play only when dealing with the out-group, the Stone Soup. After explaining all this, Sam turns a critical eye on his own participation in the simulation; in the excerpt that follows he is discussing the day that he and his group traveled to Stone Soup territory to trade.

> My approach to trading seemed very bold and Americanized in comparison to the two Korean girls in my trading company. After going back and forth in their game (on the day we went on our trading trip) and not really making any money, I just outright asked the Stone Soup members if I could have some money and they happily gave me money from each of their stacks. They kept giving me their money until they had none to play with. They asked for some back and I did give them some, and so we continued playing the game. I was definitely aware that I was exploiting their culture and their openness and happiness. Despite the exploitation the competition pushed me to maximize my profits at their cost. I can certainly see why certain cultures were so eager and quick to exploit other cultures that were generous or held different values. Though my actions went uncriticized by Stella and Jade, I didn't feel 100% good about it, but I was certainly admired and adopted by the white members of my culture that saw my actions and followed suit. (Sam, FT, 4/29)

Money, Money, Money Makes the Simulated World Go 'Round, Too

Many of the Traders reported a growing disdain for the Stoners—seeing them as "spoiled, because they don't need to work for their money. Everything is just handed to them." (Travis). Just as many confessed that they felt ashamed of the ways the Traders had "fallen so easily into the role of ravenous, rapacious, insatiable sharks" (Anna). In the field notes the class appeared fairly evenly divided on this, but as soon as the bell rang and trading began, all that shame gave way to the hunger, and the feeding frenzy resumed. We could only assume that prior to the simulation, money, or the meaning that the students attached to the idea of money, was somewhat consistent across the two cultures, but at this point in the simulation this was no longer the case. The two cultures had transformed their attitudes toward money in vastly divergent ways.

Although it was strictly forbidden in the original trading instructions, the Traders now openly admitted that they had been making agreements within their small groups whereby no two players would attempt to collect the same color of cards, and surreptitiously trading within their own small groups until each player had all of the group's inventory of one certain color, red, for example, and had relinquished all differently colored cards to others in their group. Anna shares her trading strategy below.

> Due to my success from the prior trading practice I was extremely excited this time around. My strategy was to trade within my own group before trading with those in other groups, since there was no point in two members in our group trying to accumulate the same color of cards. Once I had what I needed from the other members of Bella Trading Company, I was on the prowl looking for the other cards to fulfill my set. I kept my eyes open for 3's and 5's that are rare. I charged at only the other Traders that had the color I needed. Adrenaline pumped throughout my body as I anxiously hunted down the cards I needed. And in no time at all I had already cashed in my straight for $100 and a brand new set of cards. Before I knew it I was back at the bank trading in another straight for another $100 and some more cards! There was no stopping me! (Anna, FTC, 4/29)

The Traders had performed in alarmingly money-focused ways in the simulation, but finally they were working to make sense of these actions in their nightly field notes. The dominant reasoning went something like this: the Traders' first priority was to perform as successful members of the Cartel; that entailed being fair in all things, honest yet openly competitive, law abiding yet aggressive. The problem was that in their efforts to be all these things, the Traders found themselves in situations where it was in their best interests to take unfair advantage of the Stone Soup culture. What exactly constituted an unfair advantage was questionable since no explicit rules detailed how to trade with outsiders other than the admonition to always trade only in the Traders' language, which, of course, the Stone Soup members were not able to speak.

The Stoners, even those who had been most generous in their evaluation of the Traders earlier in the game, described them now as *"motivated by money alone," "consumed by the need for money,"* or *"focused on only money."* Some of the Stoners took it on themselves to try and teach the *"cash-crazed foreigners,"* as Jason liked to call them, about money's proper place in life. Sailer's story shows how fruitless these efforts were.

> One visitor kept just randomly taking money from the pot for no reason. We just ignored her and continued our conversations about our grandmothers as much as we could. They were leaving and we took a group picture and then it was Elliotte's (our treasurer's) idea to give them their own currency back—to try in some way to show them that we valued their company, not their money. We had 1's and 50's so we put the 50 dollar bills into the middle of a stack of 1 dollar bills to surprise them. "If we could only see the looks on their faces!" Elliotte said as we gathered the stack together. Since she couldn't talk to them (she was the treasured one), I said I would say they were from her, but then I just ended up handing our visitor the stack and saying "thanks for coming!" Even though they didn't play according to our rules too well, they still deserved a parting gift. But after all that, she still took our coins for herself too, sooo ;. . . ." (Sailer, SS, 4/29)

When it became clear that the Stoners were never going to decipher the Traders' language or the rules of trade, a few Traders lost their appetite for Stoners' blood. "It's just too easy." "It's starting to feel wrong. I wish we could have let them in on some of the rules." The playing field was so unbalanced that the game lacked sport. But the majority, as Anna indicates in her notes, acknowledged the unfairness of it all and then went along with the exploitation anyway.

> I did in fact today take full advantage of the Stone Soup members trying to earn back my high trading status. When I simulated motions for them to give me their currency I knew what I was doing. I knew their currency is valued at a much higher rate than the Fair Trade currency. I did not trade with them to help them. I did it out of greed to try to secure my financial success. Clearly in this action alone you can witness the different moral values of the two cultures. It's kind of bizarre how

the mentality of the Fair Trade culture to make money had overtaken my own personal values, at the end of this experiment I was not thinking like Anna. I was thinking as a Fair Trade Cartel member. (Anna, FTC, 4/29)

Here I take the lead from Barab and Plucker (2002) to think about the ways our thinking and behaviors emerge and are maintained in social context. These authors suggest we think in terms of a contextualized self that, through exposure, becomes sensitive to the structures and norms of the groups or organizations to which it belongs. Using this model, context is as much about social relationships as it is about location and material artifacts. In Michael Cole's words, context is "that which weaves together." This definition emphasizes the coconstitutive nature of social events—the ways that ideologies, artifacts, institutions, and individuals come together such that particular patterns of activity emerge (1996, 135–37). Context, so defined, becomes an integral part of our cognitive processes. In the language of Gary Alan Fine (1987) and Frederic Bartlett (1932), a group's idioculture and its members' previously acquired schemas come together in what Barab and Plucker (2002, 165) call the "individual-environment transaction"—that is, in a contextualized individual who internalizes local influences and procedures and creates specialized responses.

The Traders and Stoners alike were maneuvering between remaining true to the spirit of their simulated cultures and faithful to their personal belief systems while meeting the academic demands of the class. The simulation was compelling, but the fact remained that this was all taking place within a graded university course; when choices had to be made between acting in accordance with culturally acquired inclinations about how to behave in certain social situations and acting in ways that might improve the chances of a good grade in the class, the students faced a dilemma. Stoner Fredrick offers one great example: "My inner self and the Stoner in me just wanted to tell all of the greedy B******s to go back where they came from, and not to come back until they were ready and willing to act as if they were decent human beings. But we were not in the real world, we were in a Communication class, so I knew we had to hang around and communicate." Trader Anna offers another: "Truthfully, I could not see any reason why we had to build relationships with the Stoners at all. We had our society and our jobs to do and they (the Stoners) just got in the way. Okay, Okay, I know that I'm missing the whole point of the class. It was just hard to remember the class was real and the game was not."

Indeed.

I was looking forward to the next phase of the project where the students would move from being embedded ethnographers to being reflective researchers who were analyzing their collected data. In my mind the simulation was now over. I fully expected that once the students had an opportunity to collectively step back and reflect on the events, they would see each other once again as classmates and would return to their original levels of respect and tolerance for each other. They might even feel closer and kinder now that they had gone through so much together. I was mistaken. I was about to discover that the "simulation" had been over for weeks. While many of the activities had been contrived, our involvement in them and the feelings that involvement invoked were far from simulated. They were very real. Moreover, our emotional engagement and the intensity of our interactions would escalate as we moved forward, coloring our thinking and influencing our behaviors in ways that I could not have predicted.

PART 4

The Unreconciliation

May 6th: Stupid, Boring Hippies

The simulation portion of the course was complete, and for the remainder of the quarter the two cultures would convene as a single class. Our plan was to spend the first two days "unpacking" the events of the last five weeks. For the first of these classes the Traders had prepared a short presentation, reporting all they had learned or surmised about the Stone Soup culture during the simulation. The Stoners would then offer a more comprehensive account, telling about "life as it really was" in the Stone Soup world. Before we began we encouraged all members of the class to interrupt with questions or comments. The idea was for the integrated group to have an open, honest, and hopefully fun and informative dialogue of discovery about the simulation they had just completed. The next class meeting was to follow exactly the same format, the only difference being that the Fair Trade culture would be the topic of conversation.

Stoners Claim the Moral High Ground

We were to meet in the same large conference room that had been the Stoners' home for the past five weeks. The night before I had arranged the tables and chairs into a forward-facing U shape, with additional seating along the back and side walls. This morning I arrived to find the door locked and the students congregated in the hall. When I unlocked the door they filtered in, the Stoners clustering in the approximate areas of the room that had been occupied by their families during the simulation. This left the chairs along the back and side walls available for the Traders.

Rachel was immediately aware of an overt display of "your teacher–my teacher" behaviors from the students as they entered the classroom. The Stone Soup students greeted Rachel and Professor Mike, but ignored me. The Traders ignored Rachel. At first Rachel chalked this up as an interesting but predictable holdover from the simulation, but as soon as everyone was seated and she realized that she and I had only greeted "our own kind" as well, she shared her concerns with me. We spoke quickly about what we should do, but on the spot, we did not come up with any ideas about how to move past this. For the time being Professor Mike occupied center stage, and he had a fairly even relationship with the two cultures.

The Stoners sat quietly and appeared wary. (Later they confessed to how intimidating they had found this first session to be.) It did not help that when the class started at 8:10 A.M., a full third of the Stone Soup students were absent, while all but one of the Traders were present. This lopsided attendance, combined with the way the seating arrangement developed, meant that the Stone Soup families found themselves huddled in small groups, outnumbered and encircled by the Traders.

After the initial class business was attended to, a group made up of one member from each of the four Trading teams stood at the front of the room and began to share their observations about the Stone Soup culture. "First of all, you're all a bunch of hippies." "You like to do arts and crafts and sing and dance, but you don't really need to work for anything." "You are always friendly and nice to each other." "You have some sort of fixation with your grandmothers." "You cook a lot of imaginary soup." This provoked a wave of derogatory laughter from their fellow Traders. When they came to the subject of the Stoners having vacated their homeland for a day, the Traders fired a number of questions at the Stoners in rapid succession: "Why did you leave?" "Where did you go? What did you do there?" "Did we offend you with our disrespectful use of the word 'grandma'"? "Were you angry because we wouldn't teach you our language?" "Were you frustrated because we wouldn't teach you how to trade successfully in our territory?" "Were you upset because we blatantly wanted to take money from you when we visited your country?"

The Stoners did not answer these directly, but reluctantly began to offer information about their cultural practices. After considerable urging from Rachel, one of the Stoners haltingly read the Stone Soup legend aloud. Others joined in and talked a little about their daily activities. They told of the cultural leak, being careful not to incriminate any of their own. They explained orchestrating the "hurricane" so that they would have a chance to regroup. They discussed their worry that the Traders would steal the Stone Soup fortune and their decision to "bury" it to keep it safe. This prompted another staccato barrage of questions from the Traders: "But you said the money didn't mean anything to you." "If that was true, then why did you care?" "Why did you hide it?" "Why did you replace it with less valuable coins?" And the unkind observation: "You say one thing but you act out another."

When the Stone Soup disclosed the rules of their initial card game, the Traders rolled their eyes and groaned about how "stupid and boring" Stone Soup life had been. They then fell back into the old line of questioning: "If winning was not important to you, and you could see that it was important to us, why didn't you just let us win all the time? . . . and give us all your money?"

The Traders asked no questions at all about the Stoner's social structure, about the family units, or about daily life in Stone Soup territory, but the Stoner's first response was to present a large pictorial map—a sort of family tree that they had created before class. At the center of the poster was a large symbol, USS for United Stoner's Soup. Around this the students had added drawings and cutouts that depicted the different Stoner families as well as some of the objects and values that the Stoners held dear.

"Holy Sh**!" Trader Bruno muttered to those around him, "My third grade sister makes stuff better than that." His buddies guffawed in agreement. I shushed them and hoped none of the Stoners had heard. "Come on, Prof," Bruno whispered to me, "This is college. You gotta admit . . ." I shushed him again.

As the Stoners began to speak with an increasingly defensive voice, they also began to fabricate stories on the spot (we learned later) in response to some of the Cartel's questions. Jason makes the following observation in his notes.

They were asking questions that we had not really thought about. It was funny now to see Dennis and Melissa making up answers as if they were true. What was really interesting was that, at the time, when I heard the things they said, I believed them too. I guess it was because they said almost everything we did, even if we made it up in the simulation, was "passed down from our ancestors." We all got confused about the money and where it came from and where it went and where the new money came from and what the money was really for. I think we must have sounded dumb to them because in the Cartel there was no confusion about money. It was every-thing. It was their God! (Jason, SS, 5/6)

My notes from this day indicate that I was frustrated with our inability to get the Stone Soup students talking, and I was placing all of the blame on the Stoners for not being sufficiently engaged. My feeling was that there was so much they should have been telling the Traders. They should have been passionately and persuasively defending their lifestyle, but they could not even get the conversation off the ground. I felt they were not trying hard enough. I am embarrassed now to include the following notes.

The Stoners were maddeningly reticent today. They just don't seem to care if the rest of us ever understand Stone Soup culture or not. I guess it didn't help that when they did open up a little, their comments were greeted with derisive or dismissive responses from the Traders, but the Stoners really need to make some effort—-they need to jump in and explain themselves. I am so annoyed with that morally superior vic-tim's stance that they are assuming. Poor them! Of course, the Traders ARE pretty arrogant. I have this uncomfortable premonition that we will never be able to successfully blend the two groups into a single community of learners. It takes two sides to make this work. We can't do this alone. The Stoners are going to have to step up to the plate. (Deborah, 5/6)

Rachel's notes from that day did nothing to alleviate the sinking feeling in my stomach, but they provide a good account of the Stoners' predica-ment. Note her repeated reference to "my" students:

The Traders asked their questions. . . . . I looked at my students in the center of the room—surrounded, literally, by the Traders—and asked who would like to go up first to talk. I nudged each family to volunteer somebody, and we wound up with Dennis, Aaron, Mama C, Melissa, and Mandy. I had nudged

Jasmine but she didn't want to go up—and the rest of the Connections family was just trickling in so I didn't want to send them up clueless.

They looked at me a bit panicky, as if unsure where to even start, so I urged them "just tell them what our culture is, what we value, and then maybe tell them about our daily routine." And they still seemed unsure. "Maybe start with why we call ourselves United Stone Soup?" This started them rolling. Dennis said he'd like to draw on the board, and Melissa said "ah but we have the map with us!" All of those up front brightened a little, and throughout the room several of the Stoners smiled—in memory? Dennis then showed the flag and Mandy, Melissa, and Mama C all fiddled with the map to show it.

Dennis explained the Stone Soup symbol, emphasizing we are a "clan." He showed them how it said "USS, which stands for (he seemed embarrassed at this point) United Stone Soup" and said it came from our soup story, hence all the discussion of soup. He then explained that each family's symbol was also on the map—and showed each one on the USS Legend. Melissa jumped in at the castle and said "Mama C lives in a castle!" which got a few smiles and slight chuckles from the room. Then they haltingly started to tell about the values "We value each other, kindness, friendship. We tell stories and are just together and have fun. We value sharing." Deb had Dennis read the Stone Soup story, which he did almost in a storyteller fashion. They then talked about our feast and how it was the annual celebration of our stone soup.

They told the Traders how the game was about communicating with each other, not the game itself. Money didn't matter, so it didn't matter where the coins accumulated, and they would just drop them in the pot at the end of day anyway, so what did it matter? They said each family did use different strategies for the game, and the face cards were used to show somebody they were not sticking to the values of USS. It was to guide them. Aaron held up the index card and said we accumulated signatures/initials when we played according to values, and numbers if we strayed. They were careful to point out that even other family or Stone Soup members could also get the face card or numbers. They talked a bit about their dancing, that they start the day with it, and although it seemed awkward and "stiff" at first, they really got into it and had fun. Mama C pointed to Melissa and said "and this one here got really into it on the last day!" Melissa laughed and the Stoners smiled and giggled throughout the room thinking back on it. My laptop won't export video to the CRT, but I had a slideshow of their pictures playing during the last part of the discussion.

The hurricane became a huge topic, as my students looked to me for nudging on what to say. I suggested they start with the e-mail I sent around. And Dennis said "Our cultural values, our rules, some of it was leaked. And you guys knew. Like our treasured ones. You guys knew about them" and they jokingly pointed at Loretta. They said they went to "higher ground" in the chemistry research building, where we talked about our rules and what we could do differently. There they decided on different ways to play the game and to have a protector of the treasured ones. They also told the Traders they were "Freaked out" and "Scared" by them. One of the Traders— perhaps in confirmation of their suspicion that the Stoners left out of fear— asked, "really, so you were scared?" And Dennis said "Yes! We were totally freaked out, you guys were all up in our faces and yeah we were scared!"

Throughout their explanations, my students happily pointed out the people who had stolen the coins, who asked for everything in sight, who had weaseled out information about the treasured ones, who wanted to take the treasured ones' beads, everything. My students did it in a very friendly manner, but I saw a few of the Traders seemed a bit embarrassed that they were "outted." Some even shook their heads or ducked down. Deb also asked the treasured ones to explain their experiences, and they said they felt protected and strong within our group. But as soon as they went to the Traders nobody respected them. And the face card didn't work. Elliotte told us "I probably flashed my face card 30 times and nobody cared." One of the Traders in the front row nodded his head and said "yeah that stupid card doesn't mean anything to us."

Another question was where our wealth came from, and Dennis quickly came up with a story that it was passed down from our grandmothers. Mama C added earlier that our wealth was from our values of kindness and friendship and being loving, that's how we are rich. The Trader who responded it was surprising to her because one of the things they kept wondering was how the culture could sustain itself if it gave everything away. Which brings us to the fake coins. The students explained that they had "buried" their gold after the Traders had asked to take everything with them—everything! The beads, the coins, the paper, everything. So this way, they could give the Traders something to take with them, but it was "everyday" coins *that held no meaning. So they weren't losing their resources or gold in the process, but could still give freely. The Traders, at this point, seemed shocked. They realized they'd been had, in a sense. But it wasn't even a malicious act on the part of the Stoners, since their motivation was to still "give" and make the Traders happy.*

Throughout the whole process, the students were fascinating to watch. The Traders seem to have split personalities—some are very haughty in their body language. Very commanding and sure of themselves. They sat at the front of the room and cut into the conversation whenever they felt like it, or lounged in the back as if they owned the world. Meanwhile there was another personality of Traders sitting against the side wall by the door, almost seeming timid (but maybe they were just smug?) not knowing what to say. My students, on the other hand, seemed to coalesce upon themselves, seeking comfort in each other and through constant questioning glances at me. They looked almost "uprooted" from their norms, and they sought reassurance from me and from Mama C for those who were not near me. It was interesting to watch. I also noticed the Connections family—save Jasmine—sat against the back wall with the Traders due to their late arrival. (Rachel, SS, 5/6)

I was disappointed, to say the least, in the way this class meeting turned out, but I was holding on to what I know now was an unrealistic goal. The way I saw it, all of our students had been fully complicit in this research. They (we!) all knew this was fake from the beginning. I simply could not understand why we should not be able to see the two cultures for what they were: contrived, unreal, temporary, and having no meaning whatsoever for our lives outside the classroom. It was time for us to let go of our attachments to our respective *artificial* (and frankly silly) cultures, step back, and analyze our findings like proper researchers. I would try harder to get this message across at the next class meeting.

May 8th: "You're a Bunch of Moneygrubbers."

It was discouraging to see that only ten students from the Stone Soup were present when it was time for class to start (three showed up later). While absence and tardiness had plagued the Stone Soup in the beginning (a fact I attributed to the laid-back nature of the Stone Soup culture), Rachel and

I surmised that on this day the reasons were different. The last meeting had been unpleasant for the Stone Soup much of the time and torturous for the rest of it. The Traders had been unkind at best. An undercurrent of hostility threatened just below the surface of the discussions that we struggled to orchestrate. We were hoping that today, when the Traders, not the Stoners, were under scrutiny, intergroup relations would improve.

We asked the Stoners to get up and tell us what they had learned about the Fair Trade culture. No one volunteered to speak. Because there were so few Stone Soup members, Rachel asked the entire group to come to the front of the class, but only four reluctantly complied. They began by talking about some of the ideas they had come up with to explain the Fair Trade behaviors. The four Stoners understood immediately that money and the trading game were paramount and that the Traders were divided into companies rather than families, but the game itself and the language spoken during the game baffled the Stoners. In the beginning of the presentation, one of the Stone Soup members ventured a guess about the Fair Trade culture. *"We think the different colors on the cards might have corresponded to the different companies."* Two of the Traders in the back row responded with snorts of laughter—"No! You are all wrong!" and "You guys don't know anything!"—which unfortunately shut the conversation down immediately.

After considerable encouragement, the Stoners asked a few more questions about what the Traders did when they were not trading and why their interactions completely lacked niceties such as polite greetings, "please," or "thank you." The Traders explained that they were allowed to speak only "Tradolog" while trading, a language that had no words for "please" and "thank you." Then Stoner Fredrick asked whether the Traders were allowed to make up new words if they wanted to. When the Traders answered in affirmative, he followed up with, *"Then why didn't you invent the words you needed to be polite?"*

One Stoner said she had seen the description of the Fair Trade legend on my research prospectus and had Googled "parable of the talents." She spoke up now to say, *"Your legend was taken from the 'Parable of the Talents.' That's a Bible story, right?"* Although the Traders had no idea, this was absolutely correct, but before I could explain Bruno adamantly shook his head, "No way, it was NOT from the Bible!" and his fellow Traders laughed in agreement.

The Stoners should have been asking a lot more questions, but they were maddeningly silent, so we moved on to the short video that three members of the Fair Trade Cartel had prepared to explain the trading game to outsiders. In the clip two Traders acted out a trading session, while a third provided a voice-over explanation of what they were doing. The Stoners sat quietly through the film. The first "aha moment" for the Stoners was when the Fair Trade students explained that the Stoners had possessed some very rare and highly valuable trading cards. The feeding frenzy behaviors that the Traders displayed whenever the Stone Soup members came to trade made more sense now.

When asked at the end whether they had any questions, the Stoners did not immediately respond, so Trader Harry took over and began to tell about the Traders' use of the words "grandma" and "grandpa." He went on to explain that the Traders had been concerned that this practice had offended the Stoners and may have led to the Stone Soup's disappearing act. Once again, the Stone Soup was silent, but other Fair Trade members were not. "Don't misunderstand. We didn't really care about your feelings, we just didn't want you to get angry and stop trading with us. We wanted your cards and your money!"

Uncharacteristically, Professor Mike interjected, "You're a bunch of moneygrubbers." I'm ashamed to say that, being way too emotionally involved at this point, I responded angrily, "I take offense to that! We are a culture of people who strive for personal best! We have morals and rules! It's not our intention to take advantage of others. We may be aggressive, but we're always fair!" A rush of applause and affirmations arose from the Traders. The Stoners were silent, and I immediately regretted my outburst. I desperately wanted to effect reconciliation between the groups, but I was unable to stifle my own feelings at the moment. I knew that my comments would further polarize the two camps. Rachel was understandably annoyed:

> It makes the split between cultures pretty difficult when the leaders are stepping in reinforcing the "accusations" of one side or the other. I tried not to say much of anything, because when the two groups of students are trying to figure stuff out it gets even more confusing on "what" and "who" is right if the leaders start jumping in. Especially with these ideas of "work ethic" when work was culturally defined and the material rewards (money, signatures) were completely arbitrary. (Rachel, SS, 5/8)

Once everyone realized the magnitude of my transgression, all eyes turned to Professor Mike, and you could have heard a pin drop. Stone Soup member Melissa, in an obvious effort to diffuse the tension, broke the silence with a question for the Traders: *"What did you do besides trade?"* The answers: "We strategized about the game. "We planned our next moves." "We counted our money." Melissa was not satisfied with these responses, *"But what else do you do? What do you do that is not related to the trading game?"* It was the Fair Trade's turn to be silent.

Then Melissa asked, *"Some of you guys were so different when you came to visit us—so much nicer—polite even—you never seemed to want to go home. Which culture did you like better?"* Trader Travis laughed, "We didn't want to leave because we wanted to stay and get as much of your money as we could."

At this point the Stone Soup members shook their heads in disbelief. *"So it's true, the ONLY thing you cared about was money?"* This is when the discussion took an unexpected turn. The Fair Trade members began what can only be categorized as a full-fledged attack on the Stone Soup, all of them speaking at once, raising their voices to be heard over each other, accusing the Stoners of being lazy, spoiled, and without a work ethic.

Again, Rachel was rightfully concerned.

> *I didn't really like this turn in the conversation (if you can even call this a conversation) since it implied that the Stoners didn't work for anything, and reinforced a work/behavioral ethic that the Traders seemed to have an underlayer of superiority about. It seemed counterproductive to argue that one works "harder" than the other, whereas I think both sides worked extremely hard for what they valued within their culture—the Traders worked very hard for money, but the Stoners worked extremely hard to build social relationships, history, stories, and even recreate their games. The "work" was quite different in each, but not easier in either, and motivated by the cultural values in both. The money was just as worthless in the Fair Trade society as it was in Stone Soup. In both groups it was set up by a completely fictional backstory. Any of the Stoners could have opted out of the game entirely and decided not to "work really hard" for it, and they would have still reaped the same benefits of group membership (with the exception of having their name at the top of a list). Similarly, a Stoner could have—and we had some who did in a sense—opt out of the cultural values of storytelling, grandmas,*

non-competitive, etc.—and they still received the same material benefits.
(Rachel, SS, 5/8)

Thankfully, the class period, and the unpacking week, had come to an end. We were nowhere near meeting our goal of bridging the cultural boundaries we had created. In fact, the two groups had never been so far apart or so openly antagonistic. We definitely would not be entering into the next phase of our class as a congenial team of ethnographers. I was exhausted. As the students were packing up to leave I asked, "Raise your hand if you feel like you've been placed in a culture that is totally wrong for your personality." Only one member of each group raised their hand, but one more, from the Stone Soup culture, wrote in his field notes that he might have been happier in the opposite culture. The majority of the students were so thoroughly enculturated at this point that an impartial analysis of the simulation activities or the roles we were playing in these activities was impossible.

Student Field Notes from the Unpacking Days

I am amazed at how everyone participating in the discussion was speaking in the voice of his or her simulated culture. Every time a Stoner opened their mouth, they reflected Stone Soup values, and every time a Trader spoke, it was with the best interests of the Fair Trade culture in mind. I did it too, and sometimes I got real heated up about it. This was fascinating to me, because we've absorbed the values of our respective cultures through our very skin, and during the somewhat heated discussion, we were each valiantly defending our own cultures. By the end of Thursday's class, I was even more annoyed with the Stoners than I'd been the previous week. I think it's because the Fair Trade culture reflects the values I already have: hard work and competition and striving to reach goals. The Stone Soup culture is the leisure culture, and if I had to sit around all day and play cards and talk to people, I would go insane with boredom, and I would have absolutely no self-respect. I believe that leisure time should be earned, and in fact I was bored when I visited the Stone Soup culture, but I didn't let it show because I was being polite. I wasn't surprised at all when they said the card games were essentially pointless—I'd already sensed that, and when they explained the grandmother system, I realized that I'd guessed that too.

There was a girl in a pink shirt from the Stone Soup culture who was incredibly anti-Traders. She thought that our competition for the Starbucks card was silly and that our values were askew, that we shouldn't value money over friendship, etc. She called the Traders greedy several times. I raised my hand and pointedly said that if the Stoners actually had to earn their money to survive, they would feel differently. She countered that the Amish were able to live very simply and didn't need to earn money. I was at the point of asking her if she'd actually like to be Amish, but I held my tongue because I didn't want to insult any religion like that. It's easy to value friendship and socializing when you don't have to eke out your own living. I very much doubt that she'd actually like to be Amish and thought that her even bringing that up was ridiculous. It's pretty obvious that I would not like to switch cultures. I don't think the Stone Soup culture is remotely sustainable. As wonderful as it sounds to have money in the communal wealth pool from generations past, that just sounds incredibly unrealistic. Money runs out unless it is replenished in some way, and the Stoners take no steps to replenish their funds. Not only that, but they give it away in bundles. If we'd carried on the simulation they would have eventually run out of money. This is not to say that Stone Soup doesn't have its fine points. It's good to relax and unwind and socialize with friends. Traders need more of that, but the Stoners also need to find other ways to pass their time, because as of now their culture sounds rather boring and Communist. They said that individuality is valued and I respect that, but there needs to be competition and the building of an economy in order for their society to be sustained. They all act as if they're in retirement, a retirement that they didn't earn. I do feel bad that they felt uncomfortable and mistreated when they visited us, and I expressed this regret in class. But I also prefer my culture, because I feel as if the Stoners are just lazy, and as an individual I don't like laziness, nor do I like the idea of mooching off some communal pool of money instead of earning my own way through life. (Ally, FTC, 5/8)

We Stoners are stronger in morals. (We have morals!) We treasure each other more which makes us more of a peaceful society, not needing to deal with certain disputes The Fair Trade culture involves itself with such as cheating and stealing and exploiting others to increase their own wealth— which really means nothing because it is not even real money. I personally like Stone Soup-like society more, one that's somewhat "communist" in its dealings with possessions. I like how each individual shines according to their own personal life stories ("How is your grandma?") rather than through their value as a selfish and thoughtless Trader. There is no need for incentives for we are already thriving and therefore no one is being taken advantage and there is no economic disparity that results due to such an aggressive economy. I have a huge heart for the poor, so naturally I'm drawn to any conclusion that is able to elevate the lives of a large population of poor and disadvantaged people.

The Traders lacked culture and morality and I felt very sorry. They educated us through their very cold and high tech manner of video and reenactment. They had nothing in terms of family values and the activities I would have expected them to present did not exist. If we could go back to living our separate cultures after this discussion, I think the Traders would eventually have realized that they had been gypped. In another week or so, I could have speculated that their game would have gotten old and then where would they have turned? They would have nothing but their own selfish desires to steer them. The interaction between the Stoners and Traders served to show this stark contrast. In my mind the difference between us was always vast, but now that we know them better the gap has grown even farther apart. They are Traders and we are Stoners. (Jessica, SS, 5/8)

Rachel, Mike, and I met after class to discuss how to proceed. Although I desperately wanted and needed their advice, I talked and talked (ranted and ranted), never letting either of them get a word in, until they both politely excused themselves and left me alone with my frustrations. Below is a portion of my notes from that meeting.

Oh, God. This project has taken on a life of its own. It's running away with me! Rachel hates me (understandably) and Mike is trying to decide how much rope to give me ... enough to hang myself? They make me crazy. The whole thing makes me crazy. Did I really believe I could set an endpoint for the two cultures? It honestly never occurred to me that their (MY!) group loyalties would continue past the simulation. I had such a well-laid-out plan. AAAGGGHHH! Right now we should be looking back on the simulation experiences in awe and amazement at what we accomplished together. We should be examining our mountains of rich and detailed data, sharing insights, planning how best to present our results. Instead we are fighting over which culture was the best. That was never in question. There is no best. Was I naïve? Or what? I need to get this under control! I need to get ME under control. Prioritize! Prioritize! The class comes first. I need to rescue the class first (I only have three weeks!) and then try to make some sense of the research project later. I guess I've learned one important thing—the hard way, of course—*you can't undo culture.* (Can that be my research findings?) I keep thinking about that angel of progress.[10] What are we leaving in our wake?

May 13th: We Are We, and They Are They

Goethe's scientific method involves three stages of discovery (Goethe 1988b). The first is the *identification of an empirical phenomenon.* In our case the phenomenon was defined when the experiment was conceived; we wanted to experience the genesis of culture in small groups of people. Goethe's second stage is to attempt to *replicate that phenomenon under different conditions from those in which it was originally observed.* At this point I firmly believed that we had accomplished stage two through the cultural simulation game. We had developed two new and totally different social systems, each with its own framework for making meaning of the class events. We had each identified strongly with one of these systems and labeled members of the opposite culture as "Others." We had developed complex practices for the express reason of constructing boundaries between the two groups, and we were now expending considerable energy to sustain and negotiate these boundaries.

Goethe's final research stage is to recognize and chronicle the *pure phenomenon* as it emerges in a continuous sequence of events (Zajonc 1998). It is this third phase that allows researchers to generalize their findings. There are two implications here. The first is that having isolated the phenomenon and experienced its development firsthand, we now have a deeper understanding and appreciation of it. The second is that should a similar sequence of events occur allowing the phenomenon of interest to emerge again, the students/researchers would be "tuned" to recognize it. In Goethe's vocabulary, we would have developed in concert with the phenomenon, fine-tuning our organs of perception to be sensitive to cultural processes. I felt our class was now in this third and most critical phase. Success or failure here would dictate what the students would take away from the class and would prescribe the form and message of my dissertation.

Our largest problem, as I saw it at the time, was that we were unable to get the distance necessary for a comprehensive understanding of the events we had all participated in. I was counting on the next phase of the course, discussions of the literature from the class reading list, to function as a sort of intervention or new beginning that would diffuse some of the emotional tension, allowing us to disengage emotionally and step back a bit. I hoped that the social theories we were grappling with would reorient or reposition us, provide us with new lenses through which we could view the ways our cultures had developed, and lead to fresh ideas about why we might be feeling and behaving in the ways that we were.

Throughout the simulation, we had been reading Guiseppe Mantovani's (2000) *Exploring Borders: Understanding Culture and Psychology*. This is a wonderful little book that weaves historical events and social theories into a highly readable narrative about the ways in which culture acts as a framework for organizing our experiences. The strategy for the next three weeks was to revisit the theories and examples that Mantovani offered, to augment them with other classic and contemporary works, and to discuss these in light of our experiences in the simulation. The students were to continue their practice of submitting written reflections after each class, but now, instead of writing field notes, they were to write commentaries integrating the course readings with the simulation events.

Each day a different group of students would be presenting the various readings to the larger group and coordinating the class discussion. My plan was to have the students sign up for these presentations, choosing to present the topics they found most compelling. I created a sign-up sheet and handed it to a student in the first row to be circulated around the room. While the sheet worked its way through the group, I took care of other housekeeping issues and fielded questions about the class format for the remainder of the term. When the sign-up sheet reached the back of the room, I asked the student holding it to read off names so that the group members could find each other and begin making plans for their presentations. When no one got up to move we realized that not only was there absolutely no integration of the two cultures within these self-selected groups, but for the most part the groups consisted entirely of members of a single Stone Soup family or Fair Trade trading team. I was immediately angry at myself for not having hand-sorted for integrated groups, but the students were actually behaving civilly toward each other for a change, and we didn't want to do anything to rock the boat; so we let the group arrangement stand and moved on to the next part of the class.

The next task was to recap the first few chapters of *Exploring Borders,* where Mantovani revisits some of the historical accounts of Columbus's initial exploitive encounters with Caribbean natives. The students (still sitting with their presentation groups) were given a few minutes to review the Mantovani readings and their notes before I asked for volunteers to tell us what stood out for them; which of Mantovani's observations did they find particularly applicable to the cross-cultural encounters of our simulation?

"The Stoners were the backwards natives." "They were clueless." "They didn't know how to protect themselves from the Europeans." It was hard to tell from the Traders' comments when they were talking about the Caribbean natives and when the Stone Soup culture. They were clearly seeing one reflected in the other. It was interesting that none of the Traders made any mention of seeing themselves in Columbus's crew (although some did later in their field notes). The Stoners, however, made the Trader/Columbus connection immediately and took the Traders' blindness to it as further evidence of the similarity between the Traders and Columbus's men.

Dennis (Stoner) claimed that the Stoners' experience with the Traders were, by Mantovani's definition, "cross-cultural encounters," but that those same events, as experienced by the Traders, were not. He reads from page 21, "Can we give the name 'encounter' to a situation in which the other was not taken into any account, did not speak, did not exist as a human being, had no recognized rights?"

The Traders responded with, "But you could speak! You could speak English!"

Dennis counters, *"Yes, we could say the words, but you refused to hear us because they were not your secret trading language."*

After some discussion, Jaime (Stoner) stood up and read the following passage, making it clear that the Stoners were proud to bear the "noble savage" label.

Columbus believed that he understood the language and mind of indigenous populations, from which he was in fact separated by an immeasurable distance. His inexplicable confidence reflects the difficulty Europeans had in communicating with others and in acknowledging their cultural "otherness." The development of communication requires common ground between interlocutors, ground to which they can refer in order to explore their reciprocal intentions. There was no common ground between Columbus and the Arawak, but Columbus did not worry too much about that [*Jaime stops here for emphasis and then proceeds slowly in a raised voice*], although he did not understand their language, he just *knew* that the native "kings" wished to donate to him everything they possessed. (Mantovani 2000, 20–21)

The Traders were flabbergasted. "But it was not like that at all! You *wanted* to give us your money!"

"No. You wanted to take our money, and we had no precedent for that. We had no way to stop you."

"What do you mean? You could have just said no!"

"No we couldn't. You don't understand. There was no way for us to do that."

"What? You were allowed to speak English!"

"You don't get it. Stoners are always generous, and we couldn't act like the money was important to us—it wasn't important to us."

The Traders just shook their heads, unable to imagine a repertoire of meaning different from their own. Mike suggested we were watching the old sophisticated-Western-world-meets-primitive-native-society story in microcosm, a teaching moment for sure, but we were interrupted by the clock.

I felt the reading had done half of its job; it had provided a vocabulary for the Stoners to express what they had been trying to tell us all along; there simply had been no Stone Soup social practices in place with which to interact with the Traders. The Traders' next response, "You spoke English, didn't you. Why didn't you just say what you were thinking?" helped us (the Stoners and the research team, but, most likely, not many of the Traders) to see that language was not the issue. The ethos of the Stone Soup culture, which governed the norms of interaction that had developed, prevented the Stoners from holding back the Stone Soup treasure from the Traders. The Fair Trade imperative to amass personal fortunes, and the implicit neglect of more aesthetic or benevolent achievements, precluded the Traders' recognition of the Stoners' plight. Given more time, most of the Stoners felt they would have developed better strategies to protect themselves, but this would have entailed significant changes in the worldview that they had come to cherish.

All this seems obvious to me now, but at the time I felt like the lights had been turned on and I was surprised and disappointed to see that neither this new revelation nor Mantovani's words seemed to move the Traders from their arrogant position. Instead they shook their heads in disbelief that the Stoners could be so stupid. They were not able to understand the predicament that the Stoners had found themselves in. As Bruno's following comments suggest, the Traders' experiences in the simulation had not resonated with the reading in exactly the same way as those of the Stone Soup culture had.

> There were things Traders could do which Stoners could not, and vice versa. For example, Stoners could not scheme to make more money because in their culture money has no real meaning, while in the Fair Trade culture money is everything. As some Stoner pointed out we were like Columbus trying to dominate a different culture. But Traders also acted out using the cultural map they had, we were not the community-oriented Stoners, we were Traders and our goal was to make money.
> I recollect what I said during the Stoners' flood. I, half jokingly, said that we should crush them for taking us too lightly. Maybe my comment was not too off from Traders' way of thinking. If we had more time we would probably crush them now. (Bruno, FTC, 5/15)

In chapter four of Mantovani's book, he compares the experiences of Alvar Nunez, the Christian Spanish *conquistador*, with those of the Daniel Defoe hero, Robinson Crusoe. Mantovani's message was that Nunez, shipwrecked off the coast of Florida, naked and having lost everything, acquired a new, transcultural identity, both Indian and Spanish. Robinson Crusoe, on the other hand, having retained the trappings and tools of his original culture, dominates his exotic island. The Stoners used Mantovani's story to explain some of the Fair Trade members' behavior. They observed that the Traders were *"different people"* when they visited Stone Soup territory than they were when they stayed at home and the Stoners visited them. The Stoners commented that the Traders in their native environment ignored the Stone Soup people more often than not. When they did interact with the Stoners, the Traders were *"all alike," "pushy," "intense,"* and *"thoughtless."* Eye contact was rare, and all conversations were limited to details of the card game. When they traveled to Stone Soup country, some of the Traders suddenly became individuals with personalities of their own. Many remained calculated and aggressive, but a few were more relaxed, interested in Stone Soup culture, and even friendly. Given enough time, the Stoners surmised, these Traders might have become transcultural as Nunez did. Many of the Stoners believed they would have as well, had they been given sufficient exposure to the Fair Trade culture.

I paid closer attention to the Traders' interactions with the Stoners, looking for those friendly moments that the Stoners mentioned, but frankly, when it came to the Traders' treatment of the Stoners, what I witnessed was better described as feigned tolerance. I did notice many friendly interactions among Traders. It looked to me as though the Traders, in mixed company that included both Stoners and Traders, liked only Traders. Only when they were isolated from their own kind and surrounded by foreigners in foreign territory did they abandon their Trader ways and interact "nicely" with the "Outsiders."

The Traders were reluctant to comment on this in class, with the exception of Bruno, who once again was brash and unapologetic: "We didn't want to be one of you. We didn't want to steal from you. We just wanted to trade with you so we could make some money. Why is that so hard for you to understand?" With that the conversation moved on, but most of the Traders' field notes mirrored Bruno's sentiments. Mikelle wrote, "I don't see the importance of interacting with the other society altogether. Yes, it is an advantage to us to receive foreign money, but all we need to do is trade with them. We can get by and thrive in our own community without the cooperation of the other society." The only dissenter was Robin: "I felt really bad when the Stoners were trying to give us a chance to get to know them better and we were like, no thanks. I think we should have found a way to be better neighbors or even friends."

For the first time since the beginning of the quarter the Traders were the first to leave the classroom. Several Stoners hung around to talk, following me back to my office and staying through office hours. A week earlier I had advertised in the class for students who were interested in independent study positions for the next quarter. I was looking for participants in the simulation who could help me organize and analyze the field note database. Before the week was out, six of the Stone Soup group turned in applications. (Much later, two Traders applied.)

May 15th: Us and Them, Forever?

Our topic of conversation for the day was the classic Robbers Cave experiment conducted by Muzafer Sherif et al. ([1954] 1988). The Robbers Cave experiment brought twenty-four boys (age twelve) together in an isolated summer camp just outside Wilburton, Oklahoma, to test two hypotheses: (1) When individuals having no established relationships are brought together to interact in group activities with common goals, they will produce a group structure with established roles and norms. (2) If two in-groups are thus formed and brought into functional relationship under conditions of competition and group frustration, attitudes and hostile actions in relation to the out-group will rise and be standardized by in-group members. Sherif's work was chosen for this day's class reading, as it is quite similar in spirit and approach to our research project. The greatest difference is that Sherif and his colleagues speak from an outside observer's perspective, drawing correlations and developing theories from the informed observation of others' behaviors. Our simulation distinguishes itself by immersing the researchers in the processes we wish to understand, and giving interpretive voice to all who engage in these processes to create a multivocal insiders' account of cultural genesis.

Sherif carefully chose boys who did not know each other to assure that any results could not be attributed to preexisting issues or personal relationships among them. The twenty-four boys were carefully screened—all white, all Christian, and all from middle-class "stable" two-parent homes. They were divided into two experimental groups and matched as carefully as possible on various physical and psychological characteristics. For example, each group had an even mixture of boys who were tall, average, or short for their ages, and the boys who were known to be outgoing were divided equally between the two groups. For the first few days the two groups had no contact with each other. The boys engaged in traditional summer camp activities within their own groups: swimming, hiking, canoeing, and outdoor food preparation.

As predicted, two mini-cultures developed, each with its own name and corresponding group symbol (the Rattlers and the Eagles). A recognizable social hierarchy emerged and stabilized inside each group, as did norms of appropriate behavior. Cursing, for example, was condoned by the Rattlers, but strictly forbidden by the Eagles. The Eagles always swam in the nude, but Rattlers who forgot their trunks did not go in the water. The Rattlers adhered to a code of toughness, while Eagles cried openly and without censure when hurt or homesick. When they were told there was another group in residence, boys from both camps spontaneously suggested that some sort of sporting challenge should be arranged—a detail that is serendipitous because this was exactly what the researchers had planned to do, and significant in that it suggests a measure of in-group solidarity had occurred even before the out-groups were introduced.

The second stage of Sherif's experiment began when the boys, through carefully arranged comings and goings, "accidentally" came in contact with members of the other group during their daily activities. In a manner that suggested to the boys it was their own idea, a series of between-group contests was announced. The winning group was to receive a trophy cup, and each member would win a new penknife. The losing team would receive nothing. From the moment of the announcement, the boys never passed up the chance to insult members of the out-group. Occasionally they antagonized the out-group boys by throwing pinecones at them or defaced the bunkhouses and play areas that the other boys had so carefully arranged to their own liking.

Through a variety of camp games, which were actually skillfully designed mini-experiments, Sherif was able to document systematic and regular in-group favoritism in attitudes and judgments. In one of the games the goal was to gather beans that had been scattered over the grass. One at a time, each boy's collection was placed on an overhead projector and displayed on the camp dining hall screen. Boys from both groups estimated how many beans each boy had collected. In reality, the system was rigged so that thirty-seven beans always spilled onto the screen, but the boys did not know this, and consistently overestimated the count for their own team members and underestimated that of the out-group by a margin of about ten beans.

A surprise finding was that across more than a dozen experiments, the winning team always demonstrated the highest levels of in-group favoritism and out-group degradation. Until this point, researchers had hypothesized that increased levels of frustration would cause increased levels of aggression against members of the out-group or that the losing team would display the highest levels of favoritism and derisive behavior (e.g., Dollard et al. 1939). But in the Robbers Cave project, the opposite seemed to be true.

The Robbers Cave experiment also revealed changes inside the two groups. Sherif saw evidence early on that the boys were developing a pecking order among themselves, not so much in the way they were treating each other but in the extent to which initiatives in group activities were taken and in whether such initiatives were effective. By the end of the first week, each group had, and recognized that they had, a leader (Mills in the Rattlers and Craig in the Eagles). From this moment on, initiatives by boys of lesser standing were effective only when Mills or Craig approved them. But leadership among the boys had its limitations. Baseball was extremely important to both the Rattlers and the Eagles, but in neither of the groups was the leader also the captain of the baseball team. It was true that Mills and Craig both told their respective baseball captains which positions they wanted to play, and Sherif reports numerous instances of the two boys taking liberties in baseball and getting away with them. But when Craig of the Eagles wanted to umpire, the entire group—not just the captain—told him no, that staff should umpire, and he accepted this. He seemed to have exceeded the unspoken but agreed-on boundaries of his leadership, and he went along with the group's judgment without complaint. Off the baseball diamond Sherif found no evidence of multiple leadership. Once the group structure was established, it was stabilized and surfaced repeatedly throughout the experiment.

During the final stage of the Robbers Cave experiment a series of superordinate goals was introduced, chosen to be compelling to both groups and unachievable through the efforts and resources of one group alone. This established a state of interdependence between the groups, requiring the boys to face common problems, jointly plan solutions, and execute these plans together. In this stage the prevailing friction between the groups was reduced, and the boys became reciprocally cooperative and helpful. According to Sherif, the change in behavior and patterns of interaction between the two groups was striking to all observers; it was corroborated by the boys' responses on a written stereotype assessment measurement, which asked the boys to rate each other as either favorable or unfavorable on six different dimensions. The ratings, collected before and after the final phase of the experiment, showed both a decrease in negative stereotyping of the out-group and a decrease in positive stereotyping of the in-group.

Following the Robbers Cave experiment, Sherif (1966) reports what he believed to be the key elements of small-group formation and functioning. The first component is the identification of a common goal that fosters interactions. Those interactions must be seen to produce effects different from those the members are able to produce on their own. One example offered by Sherif was the tug-of-war. No boy could resist the lure of the competition, and individual performance was not a viable option. The second component is the emergence of a group structure and stable intragroup relationships that clearly delineate the in-group from other groups. This process is normally accomplished by the tendency of group members to fall into roles or jobs that they can perform efficiently, and it is often facilitated by the emergence of leaders who then assign roles to the less aggressive participants. The last component is the standardization of a set of norms, which regulates relationships and activities within the group, and with nonmembers and out-groups. Each of these components takes time to develop, and their strength and durability are directly correlated with the extent and the salience of the group's history.

I hoped the students in our project would be able to identify those three elements in our simulated groups and that they would take away some of the insights that Sherif articulated in his reports: particularly that our evaluations of people are based less on what they actually do than on what we expect them to do based on their own group memberships.

The Country Inc. team (Traders) was in charge of the Robbers Cave presentation. Their talk focused on the boys' intergroup relationships, particularly on both camps' denigration of the out-groups. The presenters drew a number of analogies between the Robbers Cave boys and our two simulated cultures, but they glossed over the sections of the literature that looked at the boy' initial identification with their groups, as well as those sections discussing the development of in-group relationships and behaviors.

In an effort to draw these elements into the conversation, Professor Mike attempted to display an excerpt from Sherif's book on the large screen in front of the room. When the projector balked and Professor Mike uttered a mild oath, we learned that "grandma" had also become a verb. From the back of the room a Trader shouted "grandma!" When laughter erupted, the Stoners wanted to know what had happened. Nathan explained, "Professor Mike swore, and then Harry grandma'd him."

When the fun died down and the equipment cooperated, the first thing that appeared on the screen was a passage about how quickly the Robbers Cave boys had displayed evidence of in-group favoritism. Both Stoners and Traders offered examples where their entire groups had developed strong stereotypes about members of the opposite group after hearing the brief reports of the first envoys of visitors. Aaron said, "It was pretty surprising how we formed blatant judgments about the others before we even met." Professor Mike countered with, "and all of those judgments turned out to be true, right?" An immediate murmur of agreement moved across the room, and then a pause, and then a lot of self-conscious laughter. Professor Mike smiled and added, "still not much has changed from those first impressions?" This was the single most reported event in the field notes that night. Anna wrote the following.

> Usually I'm the only black student in my class, no matter how big the class is, and the one lesson I feel I have learned from that is not to judge people by first impressions like categorizing them by skin color or nationality or anything else, so I was surprised and embarrassed to see how I had immediately judged all of the Stoners to fit the image that the Country Inc. people painted for us on the first day. When you think about it, they only met a couple of them and not for very long. So what happened was that our entire culture listened for five minutes to Country Inc.'s story about their ten minute visit to the Stoners' territory, and then we built up this big picture of what the Stoners were all about and we treated them based on that for the rest of the simulation. Wow. This is exactly what Mantovani was talking about and we are thinking about how terrible those old civilizations were, but here we are doing exactly the same thing in 2008. That's so depressing, (Anna, FTC, 5/15)

Anna's sentiments were echoed in both the Stoners' and the Traders' notes, along with musings about how much power first impressions have — even if they are secondhand, and questions about how much "truth" secondhand accounts may or may not contain. JuLi made this profound observation: *". . . and even if that was really the way the Traders had treated Jaime, how could I be sure that they would treat me the same way? And yet I didn't even give them a chance to be nice."*

Sherif wrote in detail about the power hierarchies that developed among the Robbers Cave boys, and we discussed this at length in class; so I was surprised that even though I had noticed during the simulation that one person from each of the trading houses had taken on an obvious leadership role in the Fair Trade activities, only two of the Traders made any mention of group leaders in their notes. One was Stella, who was lamenting the male-domination she perceived in her group. *"Sam suggested we should do whatever trading we could with each other before the Stoners arrived. Everyone thought this was a great idea. I had actually made this same suggestion several times before, but you know how the world works. If it doesn't come out of the mouth of a male no one really pays any attention."* The other was Travis, who wrote, *"In Country Inc. I am definitely not the leader. Mikelle takes the notes and sends us texts about the assignments. I hate to admit that Tyler is the best trader. I guess I'm the clown. I just try to have fun and make fun for everyone else."*

In contrast, several of the Stoners wrote about the well-defined roles that each member of their families had taken on. Sailer writes, *"I was not the head of our family or the treasured one, but I had a role to play and I felt at home and needed. On the day I was gone everyone said it was not the same and this made me feel good because I believed them and felt bad because I had let them down."* And Aaron writes, *"Everyone in the family has a job to do. There is Mama C and the treasured one and the one who watches out for the treasured one—that would be me."*

In class, Dennis (Stoner) suggested that one of the largest differences between the cultures was that in-group competition was a dominant feature in Fair Trade, where in-group cooperation was favored by Stone Soup. Bruno responded with, *"Yeah, we're competitive, but we cooperate with each other, too."* He pointed to a fellow Trader across the room (Mikelle, the Trader who won the overall competition in the Fair Trade games). *"Her. She and I would always trade cards first before the games started—to give* us a better chance of making a set." Several traders admitted that they had done the same. Other Traders accused them all of cheating. *"Her?!"* Stoner Melani asks incredulously. *"'Her!' You don't even know your sister's name?"* Bruno thinks for a minute, laughs, and then answers, "She's not my sister."

Trader Travis tried to explain that a sense of camaraderie had developed among the Traders, but that the Stoners did not see it. Traders Tyler and Brian, who were both on the school baseball team, added that, just like in sports, competitors in Fair Trade developed a deep respect for each other and for each other's skills. Tyler then suggested that the Stone Soup culture must have experienced *some* conflict. It had to. All of the Stoners present denied this. Stoner Dennis dismissed his family members' efforts to explain themselves, *"Don't waste your breath. All they are ever going to understand is money. Now if we could put a price on friendship they might get it."* Stoner Mandy jumped in with, *"Yeah, they might get it, but they wouldn't spend their precious money to buy it."*

May 20th: Yes. Forever.

The reading assignment for this day focused on cultural narratives, scripts, and schemas, and included excerpts from works by Morse Peckham (1965), James Wertsch (1998), and Jerome Bruner (1991). In class the students tried their best to hammer out a logical and mutually acceptable version of our story. In their field notes they were trying to craft character roles for themselves from the possibilities afforded in the emerging plot. The Traders were bent on justifying their "capitalist," "entrepreneurial," or "free market" approaches to the games. Trader Sam wrote, "This is the way the world really is. We are getting valuable experience that will help us forever. The Stoners, well, I don't know what they are getting out of this. I think they are just wasting their time. You can hang with your friends at home—no one needs to go to college for that."

The Stoners continued to occupy the moral high ground, explaining just how well suited they each were to the Stone Soup culture. Jaime wrote, *"I think this class has helped me to express the best parts of myself. . . . I'm so happy we had this chance to build a culture based on respect and kindness instead of monetary gain. This gives us all a model to strive for as we go out into the world."* Along with all this, group profiles that made sense inside the larger narrative were being redefined. Bailey, from the Love family, describes her family as the peacemakers. *"We were the ones who always tried to make everyone happy. We were the ones who did most of the special things that set the positive mood, like bringing in music and instigating a dance. Sometimes we would just spontaneously start singing 'don't worry, be happy' or 'you are my sunshine' at the table. We made an atmosphere of love and peace and happiness for the class. I think everyone thought we were hippies, and we liked that image."*

The proud strut that the Country Inc. trading group had displayed in class was now apparent even in their written work. They were not the best trading group, but nothing in their demeanors or their notes acknowledged this. Travis writes, *"We had the best team in the best culture, and we made it that way. Maybe if we had had the same people in the other culture we would have made something better out of it than they did. I think we would have. It would have been different than we have now, but I don't think it would have been wimpy like they made it."*

What sets this occasion apart from other times in our lives when similar cultural practices are undertaken naturally is that we were aware of being engaged in cultural genesis, and we were doing it in a theoretically informed manner. I had assumed that such a scientific approach would somewhat lessen the palatable emotional charge that had built up over the past six weeks, but this was not the case. On the contrary, students in both cultures had become quite expert at crafting narrow interpretations of the social theories we were engaging with, interpretations that facilitated their own emerging stories and framed themselves and their cultures in the best possible light. The result was that during this supposedly unified part of the class, the two groups not only maintained the boundaries they had established earlier but fortified them with the new theories they were acquiring.

Near the end of class Stoner Fredrick observed, *"Our culture is a lot more realistic than the Trader's. Maybe that's because we did a lot more to build a past for ourselves. We shared our histories by telling stories about our grandmothers. All of those stories combined gave us a sense of a real past. We had something to build on. You didn't. You have nothing but a bank, no real culture at all."*

Trader Sam dismissed Fredrick, "Just because you don't understand our culture doesn't mean we don't have one. You weren't there. You can't talk."

Stoner Jaime countered with, *"You wanted stuff from us, our money and our art, but you had absolutely nothing that we wanted or needed. The truth is, I feel sorry for you, because you don't have anything like what we have. How do you explain that?"*

At the time, no one tried to explain that, so I was surprised to find the following comments in the Traders' field notes.

The Stoners were complaining in class today that we didn't have a real culture. This made me think about chapter five where Mantovani has a quote regarding Alice and the Unicorn. "The unicorn views Alice as a monster because he has never seen anything like her before. Once his initial surprise is over, he easily recognizes her, provided that the recognition is mutual. Alice accepts this, and the meeting between fabulous monsters ends up in mutual understanding." (Carroll 1872 [1984], 121–24). I think maybe the Stoners are just unwilling to recognize that we have something that is just as valuable as they have. If cultures could find a mutual understanding then they would not dis one another thus solving many world problems. (Jeff, FTC, 5/20)

I was ticked off, but they had an interesting point when they brought up the issue that we have nothing to offer that they want or need. I thought that it was very rude—like it was when the Stoners just left without telling us. Alpha knew that someone from Beta was coming that day and they did not even have the decency to send someone to tell us that they had a flood or needed help. I was especially unhappy that the Bella Trading Company could not make money that day. Apart from this incident there was no real hate between Stoners and Traders until now. Now they've kind of spoiled the whole thing. In our relationship with the Stoner culture it's apparent that we are the only ones that truly benefit. If this had gone on much longer we would have crushed them, and that proves that we are the superior people. Ha. (Bruno, FTC, 5/20)

Observer Bernard added these comments.

Today the Stoners could not see that the Trader culture was just as complex as theirs. In a nutshell I saw this happening before my eyes, Peckham's dramatic metaphor. We had the directors, Rachel and Deb. The script people followed were from the founding stories and objects associated with it. And everybody that participated were the actors who played their role. Rachel and Deb provided that "skeletal structure," and from there everybody filled in the gap. Furthermore, it was the improvisation and innovation that filled in these gaps. But it was also the improvisation and innovation from these individuals that could not be predicted, but was accumulated through the progression of being exposed to the different culture. The Traders story told of being smart and working hard. They saw Stoners as just "giving away" money, so it was okay to now take it away from them. So here I am writing this coming full circle to what this class has taught me. Life is complicated! Today illustrates that someone else's culture is difficult to understand. We are saturated in our own culture, and many times we do not stop to think why we do the things we do. But, when foreign people come we realize our culture is different and we need that outside perspective to inform us that there are many different lifestyles in the world. (Bernard, 5/20)

At this point Rachel gave up on trying to help the Traders develop a better understanding of the Stoner culture, and her notes below show that she no longer saw me as her ally but as a deeply entrenched member of the Traders' culture.

Fredrick pointed out that the Stoners worked much harder than the Traders to create a shared history for themselves, but no one seemed to care about this. Again Melissa wanted to know what their culture did besides trade. Jaime echoed it, and Mike echoed it as well—what was there to their culture beside the game? The Traders seemed flustered and had no real answers.... A debate about "wealth" and work ethic came up again like it does in every class. The Traders said they had to actually work for their money, whereas the Stoners just flowed in wealth. They didn't have to do anything. After this debate, Deb told the Love family, "You guys had the cards they needed and the wealth in the money, they had to work really hard to get it." It's unfortunate that this is all any of them can think or talk about.

I do not doubt Rachel, but I honestly do not remember saying that. My own notes read as follow.

The two cultures are farther apart than ever. Both are using their own experiences to build a definition of what culture is, or what the word culture means. Both have decided that theirs is a better example of culture, and that the other is just an act, or a game, or a lesser form of culture. It seems like we are having the same arguments over and over again. I can't see how either side is ever going to change their thinking. Maybe we just need to agree to disagree and move on. Rachel is trying very hard to be nice, but I know that she is just as caught up in this as I am.

My notes from this period in the simulation are painful for me to read, and it is absolutely excruciating for me to read Rachel's comments. I did not behave in ways I could have predicted or that I am proud of now. I find it almost impossible to simply state the way I was thinking at the time. My instinct is to soften and justify my old words, but the truth is, I was a Trader, and the Traders' ethics were under attack. In our university setting, where we were steeped in a liberal academic mindset, the Traders' capitalist values were being devalued, even debased. I was angry and defensive, and things were not going to get better.

May 22nd and Beyond: The Take-Home Message

In the days that followed the students read and discussed theories about the genesis and transformation of cultural norms and artifacts. Perhaps the most remarkable thing about the remainder of the term was the extent to which the students took charge. Once it became apparent that the simulation events had been inspired by the same authors appearing on the reading list, the students clamored, literally, to share their ideas about how their experiences had, or had not, supported the authors' hypotheses. At the students' request we often delayed the class proceedings to do close readings of certain passages, after which the students engaged in animated discussions about what the authors had in mind and how these ideas applied to the Stone Soup and Fair Trade cultures.

Our discussion about Gary Alan Fine's concept of idiocultures, the systems of norms that develop in small groups, prompted several of the Korean students from Fair Trade to share their experiences with the class. Jessica and Sam both said they had learned in other classes that Koreans have a "very skewed and idealistic" (Jessica) view of Americans, believing them to be open, big-hearted, friendly, and trusting. "Koreans believe that Americans usually conduct business with a high degree of integrity" (Sam). Jessica told the class that she and her Korean friends had a terrible time sorting out their loyalties during the simulation. "I didn't even realize that I had this order set up in my head where I felt like I should be loyal first to the other Korean students, second to the Americans, and last to the non-Korean Asians." At this point Jessica apologizes for assuming that all of the Korean Traders were thinking the same way, but some of the others assured her that they had been having similar thoughts, even if they had not fully recognized them at the time they occurred.

In the discussion that developed, several Korean students (all Traders) added that being assigned to a small trading team complicated their participation in the simulation. Suddenly they found themselves affiliated with persons from several ethnicities, against teams that were equally constituted. The decision to align with a non-Korean team member against a Korean from a different team was not always an easy one to make. The team or "family" loyalty usually won out, but not without considerable soul-searching and subsequent second-guessing. In every case the students expressed surprise and regret that this had made a difference to them, and a lengthy discussion followed in which they argued about whether these feelings were unique to the simulation or were present but unrecognized in other campus interactions as well.

I was thrilled to hear the Traders sharing experiences and insights that I thought would resonate with the Stoners' experiences as well. Stoner Stephanie's response quickly disabused me of this misconception. *"Well, I'm Korean, and if I had been in the Fair Trade culture I would never, ever, have exploited other people the way you did."* Trader Bruno immediately jumped in: "You weren't there. You don't know what you are talking about!" And yet another battle broke out, but this time the fighting was between the Korean Stoners and the Korean Traders.

One of the more important topics we addressed in class was the appropriation and transformations of artifacts inside the two cultures. We introduced the classic study by Rose and Felton (1955) who were interested in discovering the minimum requirements necessary for the emergence of the rudimentary expression of certain shared experiences that qualify as cultural artifacts. Rose and Felton offered a minimal definition of culture as "the capabilities and habits acquired by man as a member of society," and brought together groups that were barely large enough, in sessions that were barely long enough, for behavioral habits to develop (Rose and Felton 1955, 383).

At each of Rose and Felton's informal small-group sessions, participants were asked to examine a collection of Rorschach-style inkblot cards and to develop a lexicon of descriptive labels for referring to the different images. Each successive meeting called for the examination and discussion of cards that had been talked about in previous sessions, allowing each person to copy (or not) labels previously created by others or by him- or herself. As the experiment progressed, the memberships of the groups were rearranged at regular intervals. This procedure allowed responses to be invented by a participant in one group, borrowed by other members of that group, repeated as a habit, and ultimately, with an interchange of group members, diffused to other groups where they might be borrowed by still other participants.

The participants' descriptive labels were categorized by Rose and Felton as *inventions* (the first appearance of the description), *culture borrowings* (repetition of a description by others in the same session it was used), *habits* (repeated use of a description by the same participant in consecutive trial sessions), and *culbits* (descriptions borrowed from others that become habits). Rose and Felton (1955, 391) found that although *invention, borrowing,* and *habits* fluctuated according to various social circumstances, once a description achieved *culbit* status its use increased relentlessly regardless of social circumstance. In other words, once a description was accepted by the majority, it was apt to remain in stable use within the group. A very revealing finding was that once a description attained *culbit* status, all innovation (novel descriptions of that particular inkblot) stopped.

Rose and Felton's method provides a narrowly controlled and focused look at cultural genesis. They isolate and focus specifically on the production and transmission of group-specific ways of categorizing and sharing information. Their findings are useful in thinking about the creation, adoption, and adaptation of culture within and between the groups that participated in this research. Like Rose and Felton's, our research focused on how new ways of communicating (words, gestures, patterns of behavior) might arise, take hold, persist, and change within small groups. Our approach differed in that Rose and Felton attempted to isolate these practices to examine and measure distilled bits of culture as they emerged in a laboratory setting; our goal was to observe these same phenomena as they emerge in a more natural setting where emotions, value judgments, and personal commitments were made visible. We hoped now that the Rose and Felton work would give us a vocabulary to talk about the artifacts that had emerged during the simulation, and a method for tracing the transformation of these artifacts as they were brought into service as circumstances of the simulation demanded.

We gave the two groups a little time to discuss Rose and Felton's work and to come up with some examples of artifact transformations inside their cultures. The Traders immediately chose the word "grandma" and drew a chart on the whiteboard showing how the word had taken on new and expanded meanings as the simulation progressed. The Stoners had a little more trouble with this assignment. They discussed the transformation of the Traders' money into jewelry but were not able to agree on how exactly that fit into the Rose and Felton logic. Finally the Stoners settled on the ways they had adjusted and readjusted the card games to make them less decipherable to the outsiders.

Rachel encouraged all of us to think about the original BaFa' BaFa' game procedures and about how these had been adopted or ignored, interpreted and deployed as the events of the simulation transpired. Following Rachel's prompting, Stoner Bailey piped up. *"Oh yeah, an example might be those cards, the kings and queens that we held up to tell the Traders they were breaking the rules."* With that she drew her hand up to her forehead as though displaying one of the censure cards. As if on cue, three of the Traders in the back row held their hands to their foreheads as well, but they were making the classic "L for loser" gesture. I was furious and glared at them from across the room. Luckily only a couple of witnesses noticed, and they chose not to comment.

We took this opportunity to suggest to the students that the phenomena we had all experienced in our simulation strongly argues for cultural historical mediation as a central process in the creation of what appears to be assimilation and accommodation as ordinarily conceived in the Piagetian literature.[11] Assimilation and accommodation are the two interactive processes described by Jean Piaget (1952) through which information from the outside world is internalized by the individual. In assimilation, an individual's perceptions of the outside world are brought into his or her internal thought processes without altering the existing meaning-making structures. In accommodation, changes are made to the existing logic structures to accommodate the newly confronted information.

We followed the students' lead and focused first on the meaning of the word "grandma" as either a beloved family member or a way of expressing disapproval with another's actions, and then followed that up with a discussion about the role of play money as either currency or object of art. Each illustrated the process of social-cultural mediation in a very striking way that shows the transformation of a social representation (family relation or money) in terms of the meaning system of the receiving culture. For this process to occur, there must be an active, imaginative transformation of the meaning that enables a seemingly common token (family relation or money) to come into common use in a group's interactions—the meaning of the token is inflected to fit the nature of the interaction between the groups.

In our case, the cultural elements were an origin story, a set of "culture-specific" activities that were consistent with the value system of the origin story, and the cultural understandings brought through prior experience by the participants. What resulted was in fact a "virtual" world. The participants were routinely opened up to new memories of old events connected with their everyday lives. And they were certainly absorbed in a world of possibilities opened up by their participation in the given idioculture. In this world of possibilities, paper monopoly money could become either a powerful measure of one culture's social success or emotionally laden materials to be manipulated into symbols intended to belittle that culture's interpretations of success.

We also called attention to the ways these social representations, in their transformed, appropriated form, can spread throughout the cultural group (grandma among the Stoners, where grandma provided the dances and the Oreos) or be used in a relatively straightforward, instrumental way (grandma among the Traders, where the word "grandma" was used to accuse players of committing a crime) in line with the idiocultural system of which it is a part.

The most sobering conclusion from these results, if in fact they are generalizable beyond the special conditions we created, is that once a foreign term has been inverted and adopted, each occasion of interaction between the conflicting parties is likely to increase the intensity of the conflict between them. Each new (doubly misconstrued) interaction is another occasion to be confirmed in one's (misconstrued) interpretation of the other.

Probing the Possibility of a Universal Understanding

The final reading for the class was anthropologist Laura Bohannan's (1966) classic article "Shakespeare in the Bush." (Those students not familiar with *Hamlet* were asked to also read Edith Nesbit's [1907] summary of it in *Beautiful Stories by Shakespeare*.) In "Shakespeare in the Bush," Bohannan reflects on time she spent with the Tiv people in West Africa. Before leaving Oxford, a friend of hers complains that Shakespeare, being a "very English poet," is difficult for Americans to understand. Bohannan protests, arguing that human nature, with only a few local particulars, is universal. Hearing this, her friend gives her a copy of *Hamlet* to study in the bush, asking for the universal interpretation on Bohannan's return.

When she arrives in Africa she is disappointed to learn that poor weather has delayed the arrival of the Tiv elders, which means the ceremonies she has come to observe have been postponed. To pass the time she joins the locals in their daily routine of beer drinking and storytelling. When she is asked to share a story from her own country, Bohannan recounts Shakespeare's *Hamlet* to the group, taking this opportunity to prove to herself and her friend that the true meaning of the story transcends language and cultural barriers.

As she attempts to tell the story of Hamlet, she is interrupted at every turn as the Tiv people question the motives and the actions of the characters. From one scene to the next, Hamlet is seen to be acting in ways that are well outside the Tiv understanding of natural human behavior, and in the end he is judged to be mad. Bohannan, hearing the story now with Tiv ears, is forced to admit that her English interpretation was far from universal.

Bohannan's account shows that all narratives are embedded within the social structures and moral frameworks of the authors; as such, they are uninterpretable or, at least, take on very different interpretations outside those original contexts. Focusing on the structural and moral elements of a narrative, and importantly on the ways these can be interpreted differently depending on the lenses we use when we interpret them, provides valuable insights into cultures and cultural differences. Following Bohannan's example, I wanted the class to use the narratives we had created as tools for revealing the cultural norms and ritualized relationships that had developed within the two groups.

The students in both groups appeared to particularly enjoy this reading and appreciate its relevance to our situation. But examples of how their previous cultural experiences might have colored their interpretations of the simulation events were not forthcoming. They did a better job of telling stories about bringing the lessons learned in this class to bear on their lives outside the course and outside the university. Stoner Jaime, for example, was a human development major who, in another class, was running laboratory experiments designed to reveal young children's understanding of visual images. After her experiences in the simulation, Jaime shared her worries with the class. *"I'm thinking now that the children's performance in the laboratory context should not be generalized to the way they think at home or in preschool. Some of the stuff in our [Stone Soup] culture means totally differently things out in the real world. Maybe in the kid's minds, the little rabbits that they see on the computer screen in the lab have no connection with real rabbits, or even pictures of rabbits that they see in their everyday lives."*

After having had a little time to process Bohannan's ideas, many of the students included some thoughtful commentary in their field notes. Dennis's notes are a good example.

I have traveled to Africa and England and interacted with people from various and diverse walks of life. I had believed that feelings of love and hate, anger and jealousy are human traits that exist as universal themes. Through this experiment I have come to question the context of universal themes, or even if they exist at all. What would cause the Tiv people to feel hate, anger, jealousy etc. and how do they interpret these feelings? Are notions of regret, happiness and love identified under separate conditions for separate cultures? What kind of research can be done to better understand these factors of the human condition? Is it even possible? I know that we were randomly assigned to our cultures and yet I try to close my eyes and think like a Trader, but I can't. I must assume that if I had been assigned to the Traders' culture I would find it impossible now to think like a Stoner. How could I ever really know what someone from a different culture is thinking in real life? (Dennis, SS)

Stoners and Traders, Alive and Well (and Fighting until the End)

While sometimes the mood in class was light, even jovial, the in-group versus out-group hostility never let up. The two groups were cordial enough to make the meetings bearable, but the class remained polarized. Seating charts, maintained from the beginning, show that, with the exception of those who wandered in late, the students always sat with their own kind. Two contentious threads wove their way through all of the class activities and surfaced as minor spats between the Stoners and the Traders several times each day. The first had to do with the Stoners' perception of the Traders as "money grubbers" (thanks, Mike!). In fact, even on the last day of class, I overheard one of the Stoners saying, *"We're surrounded by Traders, guard your money!"* The second sore point was the Traders' characterization of the Stoners as "spoiled and lazy." Take Bruno's parting comment after the party on the final day: *"You guys didn't work nearly as hard as we did. You should all get at least one grade lower than us."* Neither group could refrain from tossing these grenades into the other camp every now and then, and, of course, no attack could go unanswered.

I am fond of the following quotation by Marshall Kitchens and use it often in my teaching. He notes the inherent tension in negotiating social boundaries that pivots on the distinction between insiders and outsiders, familiars and exotics. He contends that students, to develop a better understanding of culture, must be able see their own strangeness through the eyes of others.

> They have to take on this role of alien or "Other" as a way of seeing the familiar as strange. At the same time, they need their insider status in order to understand the exotic as familiar. They have to see both difference and sameness and establish a very careful combination of both insider and outsider. . . . Without a balanced and informed perspective, the result is either a naïve celebration of one's own culture from the inside, or a shallow critique of the "Other" from the outside, both failing to achieve a sympathetic and rich understanding of culture. (Kitchens 2002, 1)

I see now that one of my goals for the project had been shaped by Kitchen's passage; I wanted nothing less than the achievement of a "balanced and informed perspective" that would provide a "sympathetic and rich understanding of culture." Unfortunately, we had not even come close. The students' notes revealed very little evidence that they had made any effort at all to take the "Others" perspective. We were, in Kitchen's words, naïvely celebrating our own cultures from the inside.

We had not achieved the balanced perspective I had worked toward, and the image I had treasured—of my students and me as coauthors of a grand narrative—had pretty much dissolved as well. We had not written a story together at all. Instead, the Stoners and the Traders had written stories of their own. The two groups never came to a shared understanding of what it meant to be a member of one culture or another. Nor had they developed a common story about what exactly had happened in the cross-cultural episodes. The Stoners had some very strong and consistent opinions about who they were as a people, and about who the Traders were as well, but these bore little resemblance to the pictures that the Traders painted about the Stoners or about themselves. Melani (Stone Soup) offers the following ideas about the Fair Trade culture.

> I felt their culture [Fair Trade] was in a kind of constant unbalance. They were always weighing the cost-benefits of the choices they made not only in reference to their trading game but also in the way they treated us and their fellow members. They rigorously defended their outlook when some of the Stoners deplored their obsession with the money, especially in referencing how they would use our jewelry gifts as part of their wealth accumulation, and how they were always trying to take as many coins as they could from us. They [Fair Trade] said that we did not understand them because we had "unlimited" wealth whereas they had to earn their money. So according to them the way in which they were organized suited the means to their end, trying to support their lives. I found it funny that they considered our wealth "unlimited." It was unlimited in the sense that we defined wealth: love, compassion, sharing, peace, etc. But they way in which they defined wealth we were not unlimited. We had enough gold coins to sustain us, but we did not wish to attain anymore. They were obsessed with gaining more and more and were never satisfied. The Fair Trade culture was very thin outside of trading. By this I mean that they spent the time only eating food or coming up with strategies for trading in the next session. Whereas we were constantly inventing new traditions and symbols for representing the ideas that we believed in, they focused all their energy into the material game that they played. So instead of focusing their behavior on the ideals of their culture as we did, they seemed to be trying to find ways in which to get ahead of their own members by staying within

an ambiguous boundary called "fairness." I think that the Traders have very little understanding that particular rituals can have much abstract meaning. They could relate to our game and our jewelry for instance, but the dances were much less material in form because they only involved human participation, and so probably seemed like a waste of time (time for them meant "money"). One Trader even described the last simulation as the "Apocalypse" which I think pertains to the fact that the prize was the end, and their culture only the means to it. I did like their value of the heroic nature of the individual and the intellectual means of their game but in hindsight my culture, the Stone Soup culture is the one I would remain in. (Melani, SS, final reflection)

None of the Traders' notes about the Stoners were as thorough, or as thoughtful, as Melani's were about the Traders. In fact, many of the Traders' field notes revealed no effort at all to understand the subtleties of the Stone Soup culture. The following commentaries, written by Sam and Nathan, are typical of those that the Traders submitted about the Stoners.

It was very interesting on the last day to see how the Stoner culture still viewed our business hustle style culture of the Fair Trade Cartel. Overall they still acted like true Stoners. It still seemed like a split of the Hippie culture vs. Business Wall Street style culture. Though it shouldn't be, because every person is different, it seemed that the Stoner attitude toward us was one of extreme hurt and confusion, even though this was just a simulation! I found it sort of entertaining how hurt one girl felt and continuously commented on how badly they were ignored upon entering our culture and "taken advantage of" even though they didn't understand how, or even if they actually were, since they had no under- standing or knowledge of the card game. Please! (Sam, FTC)

The entire Stone Soup culture was very overwhelmed and scared of the Traders' culture when they came to visit. The Stoners are very selfless, loving, compassionate people that value relationships with others more than personal gain. The strengths of the Stone Soup culture were their strong relationships with others and positive attitudes. Their weakness was not standing up for themselves when others tried to take advan- tage of them. I believe the Fair Trade culture suits me best because I am a very competitive person and strive to be successful in life. (Nathan, FTC)

Who Were the Traders?

In a review of the descriptives used most often in the field notes, the Traders described themselves as hardworking, competitive, independent, honest, smarter than the Stoners, and more in tune with the "real world." The Stoners agreed about the hardworking part and added that the Traders were resilient and industrious. Both cultures judged the Traders to be single-minded when it came to money, a trait that led them to be greedy and uptight most of the time. Stone Soup added that the Traders were cold and unwelcoming hosts, without interpersonal skills, and generally lacking in "culture." As a rule the Stoners found the Traders lacking in important moral values, values that they themselves displayed in abundance. *"They really don't care about anyone but themselves." "They would rob their own grandmothers." "They don't have any social life, really. Just their common love of money."*

And Who Were the Stoners?

The Stoners described themselves as peaceful, kind, family oriented, funloving, ancestor worshiping, generous, artistic, creative, open, honest, laidback, and unconcerned about money. The Traders also described the Stoners as peaceful and agreed about their generosity and lack of concern with money, but the Traders attributed this to the Stoners' naiveté about the ways of the "real world." The Traders added that the Stoners were boring, lazy, spoiled, and backward. Half of the Traders said of the Stoners, *"They think they are perfect." "They think they are better than us." "They are so self-righteous."* The other half said things like, *"I feel bad for them." "They are helpless" "They are pretty pathetic, if you ask me."*

Not only did the two cultures draw different conclusions about themselves and each other, but they each painted deeply negative pictures of the opposite culture and highly flattering pictures of their own. The stories they told about the simulation were just as polarized and surprisingly consistent within the two groups. The Stoners told a tale of an exceptionally evolved, peace-loving society (themselves, of course) that struggled to maintain its gentle ways against the invasion of a coarse and greedy band of Traders.

The Traders' tale, on the other hand, was about an intelligent, civilized, industrious group of entrepreneurs who stumbled across a hapless clan of hippies, kind and gentle, but too lazy and backward to value or protect their own resources.

An Imagined World Made Real

At the conclusion of our simulation, thirty-seven of forty students reported they felt they had been placed in the right culture for their personalities, even though these assignments had been entirely random. Our greatest success, our claim to fame, was that we had, in fact, created two distinct idiocultures. We had developed two distinct systems of artifacts and behavioral norms, which we used to make sense of the events of the simulation as they unfolded. We had displayed a capacity for in-group bias and for out-group denigration that reflected the strength of the bonds formed within the groups and the intensity of the between-group relationships that had developed. More important, we had created a multivoiced record of these accomplishments.

Following this research project we were asked repeatedly about surprise findings. On this all of us involved in the project agreed. Within the first weeks of the simulation the events began to feel unbelievably real to each of us. No one in the project predicted the intensity of the emotional investments we would be making. Anna sums up perfectly what the rest of us were also saying in our notes.

> I know that this culture and these games (somehow the word "game" sounds wrong here) were not real, but they were not NOT real either. I was really there, in that real room, holding those real cards with my real fingers. I was really doing those things, really speaking that language with my real lips. I was really having those thoughts with my real brain. (hmmm? How can I get that money?) I was really feeling those feelings of greed and frustration, and then guilt. This class has made me wonder. Where does a game like this stop and "real life" begin? Is one living inside the other? (Anna, FTC, final reflection)

Jean Baudrillard (1995) would not have been surprised. He explains that we construct a simulation because we cannot obtain the information we want from the target entity directly; so we proceed indirectly by creating a model, which is sufficiently similar to the original that we are confident it will reveal the information we are looking for. Problems arise when we begin to test the reaction of the social apparatus to our simulations. *"The network of artificial signs will become inextricably mixed up with real elements. . . . You will immediately find yourself once again, without wishing it, in the real, one of whose functions is precisely to devour any attempt at simulation, to reduce everything to the real—that is, to establish order itself. . . order always opts for the real"* (Baudrillard 1995, 20–21).

According to Baudrillard, it is practically impossible to isolate the process of simulation from the force of the real that surrounds us. For this reason the social simulation functioned perfectly as a romantic science method in this project. Not only did the game allow us to expose and manipulate the social processes we were seeking to understand, but it engaged the students and elicited feelings in ways that permitted us to draw plausible connections between events in the research setting and those we encounter in naturally occurring life experiences.

We had created and lived for a while inside an imagined world, which is exactly the way two very influential thinkers describe culture. Evolutionary psychologist Henry Plotkin (2003) titles his book on the evolution of culture *The Imagined World Made Real*. He suggests human culture can be distinguished from the cultures developed by other living things in that all of our cultural artifacts existed first in our imaginations. Lev Vygotsky had expressed the same idea almost a century earlier: "All that is the work of the human hand, the whole world of culture, is distinguished from the natural world because it is a product of human imagination and creativity based on imagination" (Vygotsky 2004).

The personal commitment the students made in the Stone Soup and Fair Trade cultures had an impact on the students' engagement in the academic portion of the class as well. Surprised at how heavily invested they had become in their fabricated cultures in a few short class meetings, the students were eager to learn how this was possible. Earlier we discussed the deliberate measures taken to establish particular affective environments or moods for the two cultures, but we were also, equally as deliberately, creating academic atmospheres.

Parker Palmer and Arthur Zajonc (2010), in *The Heart of Higher Education*, write that there are ways of teaching that create community, but these require a virtue not always found in university classrooms: hospitality. The lack of hospitality in the classroom is far more common than we may think. Even in seminar-style classes, students learn early on to keep an intellectual straight face. It is rare to hear an honest question, to say nothing of an admission of ignorance. Instead, students ask questions designed to let the professor know that the lesson has been heard and understood. Palmer goes on to say that university classes should be hospitable spaces, not merely because kindness is a good idea but because real education requires rigor. In a counterintuitive way, hospitality supports rigor by supporting community. A hospitable learning space is one where students can disagree with the professor, argue with classmates, and admit ignorance (Palmer and Zajonc 2010, 29–30).

In our research class ignorance was the starting point for all of us, and learning had less to do with acquiring a body of knowledge from others more learned than us, than with creating a body of knowledge along with other ignorant souls. It simply was not possible to remain outside the issues we were addressing. Anything we might have taught about cultural processes from a text would certainly have been less compelling than reading those texts while engaged in practices where the sights and sounds and feelings of cultural creation were inescapable elements of the educational experience.

The kind of research I wished to accomplish, the deeply embedded romantic science experience, would not have been possible in an unfriendly space, where the students could not have let down their guards enough to truly get inside the often silly activities of the simulation. This carefully arranged classroom experience also provided the time and the scaffolding necessary for the students to experience what Goethe saw as a metamorphosis. All of us who participated in this project spent an extraordinary amount of time with our phenomenon of interest, the genesis of small-group cultures. As our cultures developed we could not help but develop in concert with them. The result, once again in Goethe's words, are "organs of perception" that have been "tuned" to acknowledge and appreciate cultural genesis in ways that are qualitatively different than if we had read other people's thoughts on the subject.

The field note comments that follow were written toward the end of the quarter by Travis. You might remember him as the self-described "twinkie, yellow on the outside, white on the inside." Now, having gone through the simulation and the course of which it was a part, Travis's comments represent the kind of reflective participation that the romantic scientist considers to be the goal of the process of participatory inquiry.

> I've been thinking about everyone talking about the Traders as being the "individualistic" culture and the Stoners being "communist" (or socialist or whatever) culture. This subject always comes up when people talk about yellow and white people and I think yellow people get really tired of it, or at least I know I do. So I was thinking about the movie *The Life of Brian*. Brian was this dude who was born the same day as Jesus and he lived next door, so people were always mistaking him for Jesus Christ and following him around asking for miracles. One night he hides out in his mom's house with his girlfriend, but when he wakes up in the morning and opens his window the crazy crowd is waiting for him outside. He gets really mad and screams at them all to go away, to stop following him around—telling them that they're all individuals—that they're all different. So they hear this and they start to cheer and chant all together, "We are all individuals! We are all different!" over and over, but there's this dude in the back that says "I'm not." And just walks away. So this is my really long way of saying that I'm watching our group and we're all proud thinking we're individuals but we're really all acting just alike, probably even more alike than the Stoners are. Does that make me like the guy who walked away? I don't know. (Travis, FTC, 5/8)

Travis's work was not out of line with the reflections of the other participants, who all spoke with confidence about the theories we interrogated through our experiences in the simulation, and wrote with feeling about the changes they had experienced in their attitudes about themselves and each other, and about culture and life in general. In writing this I have realized, rather belatedly, that despite the bumps and diversions—or perhaps because of them—this was exactly the kind of research and educational outcome I dreamed of. It came about through a processes of combining theory and practice in the manner prescribed by Goethe and implemented widely by Mike Cole and numerous members of the Laboratory for Comparative Cognition. I hope I have accomplished this in a manner that the reader finds engaging, and even, perhaps, compelling.

EPILOGUE

So how to tie up the loose ends of an ongoing conversation that weaves in and around topics like cultural genesis, intercultural communication, experiential education, the creation of cultural norms, group identity, and individual and societal development? My greatest challenge in writing *The Stone Soup Experiment* has been to limit my commentary to the way we were thinking as the simulation was unfolding and to control the tendency to wind everything up elegantly in the end. Such an effort felt excessively contrived since there is nothing elegant about hundreds of pages of field notes filled with contradictory interpretations of each and every social interaction we engaged in. Culture is not often elegant, but a "hot mess," as one of my students commented when she first encountered the entirety of our data collection. A tidy conclusion—even if one were possible—would preclude the kinds of questions and conversations this work was intended to spark. It would too, in many ways, defeat the romantic science methodology and the confessional style of reporting we worked so hard to implement.

In the end, I will close *The Stone Soup Experiment* with several related issues it raises that I believe warrant more thought, more conversation, and more research, and might even lead to a bit of change in the culture of higher education. At the forefront is the importance of emotions, play, and social interaction in the process of making meaning. Jay Lemke (2013) suggests that meanings always carry feelings with them. "We do not make meaning without having some feelings about the process and its result." We feel the significance of the process and enter into it with anticipation, curiosity, boredom, or frustration. We also feel the surprise, disgust, humor, gravity, or whatever of the outcome. In addition, as we make meaning together with others, our feelings for each other, those we bring into the event and those that develop at the moment, become integral parts of the task. "Actions are being performed, meanings are being made, feelings are being produced, all in deeply interdependent ways. . . . I have found it impossible to understand the sequences of actions, meanings-made, and feelings separately" (Lemke 2013, 73, 74).

It seems to me that the correlation between the highly emotional nature of the student involvement in the Stone Soup project and the self-reported depth of the learning experiences for these same students suggests a need to rethink the long-standing mindset in higher education that emotions and logic are somehow incompatible—perhaps even contradictory—and points to the need for a better understanding of the role of emotions and social interactions in learning environments.

Related to this, I suggest that, because these intense learning experiences emerged in an environment best characterized as play, we broaden our understanding of optimal learning contexts in higher education to include settings and activities that heretofore have been considered frivolous or inappropriate. My sense is that the emotional dimension of the meaning-making process, as described by Lemke, would be highly responsive to the mood or affective dimension of the learning environment. Unfortunately, many of us have come to equate learning with work. The result is classrooms where students watch the clock and feel like they have been released from jail when the bell rings. This attitude goes a long way toward dampening the thrill of discovery and the desire for future learning experiences. But does it have to be this way? It might be that we can reap large rewards from small efforts to include in our pedagogy elements of play, both in the sense of enjoyable, unscripted activities in which students are free to interrogate and manipulate new knowledge, and in the sense of slippage or space where new ideas can take root and develop.

I believe I speak for all of us who took part in the Stone Soup experiment when I say it is our sincere desire that this conversation does not end here and that our story might inspire others to undertake similar projects—and share their stories with us. We have no idea where this conversation will take us, but together we will feel our way.

ACKNOWLEDGMENTS

I must first thank the students of COHI 130 SP2008 and my cofacilitator, Rachel Cody Pfister, who trusted me and jumped into the simulation without reservation. The Stone Soup experiment is truly their accomplishment. I hope my account of it does them justice.

This work has arisen from the genuinely collaborative efforts of an inspired group of colleagues, all working in the purview of the most romantic scientist of all, Michael Cole. My colleagues at the Laboratory of Comparative Human Cognition, Camille Campion, Beth Ferholt, David Gonzales, Ginny Gordon, Robert Lecusay, Ettienne Pelaprat, Tamara Powell, Ivan Rosero, Stefan Tanaka, and Greg Thompson, have all spent a disproportionately large number of their weekly lab meetings listening to my rants and digressions, talking me off ledges and through the ideas that fueled the discussion above. I am deeply grateful to this stimulating, collaborative, and nurturing group of friends and colleagues.

To the members of my dissertation committee, Tom Humphries, Jay Lemke, James Levin, Hugh Mehan, and Carol Padden, who have been consistently generous with their time, their expertise, and most important, their goodwill, I cannot thank you enough.

I am grateful to my editor, Elizabeth Branch Dyson, who saw potential in a very rough draft and provided just the right amount of direction and support. I thank Lisa A. Wehrle for her skill and patience in copyediting the manuscript. And I would like to express my appreciation to the anonymous readers, whose thoughtful and insightful suggestions have greatly improved this book.

Finally, thank you to my dear husband and my precious family, my refuge and my heartbeat, for the things they have done, and especially for the things they have done without, to support me in achieving this work.

NOTES

1. Translation from Steiner (2000, 212).

2. A wealth of information available on the web describes the BaFa' BaFa' social simulation and its applications. The following links and reference are good places to start: "Simulations for Schools/Charities," Simulation Training Systems, accessed November 19, 2014, http://www.simulationtrainingsystems.com/schools-and-charities/; Garry Shirts, "BaFa' BaFa': Train the Trainer," 2009, https://www.indstate.edu/diversity/docs/Bafa-Diversity-10-01-09.pdf; and Garry Shirts, "Cohesion Through Diversity Presentation Before the Indiana State Office of Minority Health," Minority Health Conference, August 21, 2009, http://www.simulationtrainingsystems.com/wp-content/uploads/2014/04/Cohesion-thru-Diversity.pdf.

3. The following is from bible.org (https://bible.org/seriespage/parable-talents-matthew-2514-30-luke-1912-28). "Therefore stay alert, because you do not know the day or the hour. 14 For it is like a man going on a journey, who summoned his slaves and entrusted his property to them. 15 To one he gave five talents, to another two, and to another one, each according to his ability. Then he went on his journey. 16 The one who had received five talents went off right away and put his money to work and gained five more. 17 In the same way, the one who had two gained two more. 18 But the one who had received one talent went out and dug a hole in the ground and hid his master's money in it. 19 After a long time, the master of those slaves came and settled his accounts with them. 20 The one who had received the five talents came and brought five more, saying, 'Sir, you entrusted me with five talents. See, I have gained five more.' 21 His master answered, 'Well done, good and faithful slave! You have been faithful in a few things. I will put you in charge of many things. Enter into the joy of your master.' 22 The one with the two talents also came and said, 'Sir, you entrusted two talents to me. See, I have gained two more.' 23 His master answered, 'Well done, good and faithful slave! You have been faithful with a few things. I will put you in charge of many things. Enter into the joy of your master.' 24 Then the one who had received the one talent came and said, 'Sir,

I knew that you were a hard man, harvesting where you did not sow, and gathering where you did not scatter seed, 25 so I was afraid, and I went and hid your talent in the ground. See, you have what is yours.' 26 But his master answered, 'Evil and lazy slave! So you knew that I harvest where I didn't sow and gather where I didn't scatter? 27 Then you should have deposited my money with the bankers, and on my return I would have received my money back with interest! 28 Therefore take the talent from him and give it to the one who has ten. 29 For the one who has will be given more, and he will have more than enough. But the one who does not have, even what he has will be taken from him. 30 And throw that worthless slave into the outer darkness, where there will be weeping and gnashing of teeth'" (Matt. 25:13–30).

4. In this classic children's game players count aloud to three, each time raising one hand in a fist and swinging it down on the count. On the third count the players change their hands into one of three gestures: rock, represented by a clenched fist; scissors, represented by the index and middle fingers extended and separated; or paper, represented by an open hand. The objective is to extend a hand gesture that defeats that of the opponent. Wins and losses are resolved by the following rules: a rock breaks scissors; scissors cut paper; paper covers rock. If both players choose the same gesture, the game is tied and the hand is repeated.

5. Tajfel's research looked at the minimal conditions necessary to provoke in-group versus out-group behaviors. In experiments where division into groups was determined randomly (e.g., by a coin toss or drawing of straws); where no social interactions, either within or among groups was permitted; when participants had no reason to expect that they would ever interact with the others again; and where no instrumental link between an individual's responses and their self-interest existed, Tajfel's results showed a clear and consistent pattern. Subjects identified with their groups, preferring members of their own group over all others, judging them to be superior on all measures tested, and favoring them with rewards, often at their own expense. (See Tajfel et al. 1971; Billig and Tajfel 1973.)

6. This practice seemed to slightly increase Alpha involvement until the cultural exchange began, but it never really took hold. The use of the cards quickly dwindled off, and they were forgotten by week three of the simulation.

7. Use of digital cameras and recorders were not discussed prior to the visit. While we were happy to have the additional documentation, we had not anticipated the students' use of these during the visits and so were surprised to see mention of them in Jason's notes.

8. As the Fair Trade Cartel dealt with their thief, I noticed that in each of the four small trading teams one person took the lead in presenting and defending his or her team's position. Mikelle, Sam, Bruno, and Ally asserted themselves as the chief spokespeople for their trading houses. In this role they often overrode or silenced the voices of their colleagues. Bella members Jessica and Ruth, for example, felt strongly that Stone Soup should have the right to put Tyler on trial since the crime had taken place in Stoner's territory, but once Bruno had made up his mind that this was not in his best interests, he shut them down each time they tried to speak. These "leader-

ship" roles persisted throughout the simulation and even into the classroom sessions when the simulation was over.

9. Hisako is Japanese.

10. Walter Benjamin (1968, 259–60), in his *Ninth Thesis on the Philosophy of History*, describes the angel of progress like this: "A Klee drawing named 'Angelus Novus' shows an angel looking as though he is about to move away from something he is fixedly contemplating. His eyes are staring, his mouth is open, his wings are spread. This is how one pictures the angel of history. His face is turned toward the past. Where we perceive a chain of events, he sees one single catastrophe that keeps piling ruin upon ruin and hurls it in front of his feet. The angel would like to stay, awaken the dead, and make whole what has been smashed. But a storm is blowing from Paradise; it has got caught in his wings with such violence that the angel can no longer close them. The storm irresistibly propels him into the future to which his back is turned, while the pile of debris before him grows skyward. This storm is what we call progress."

11. See Piaget (1952).

REFERENCES

Abbott, H. Porter. 2005. "The Future of All Narrative Futures." In *A Companion to Narrative Theory*, edited by James Phelan and Peter Rabinowitz, 529–41. Oxford: Blackwell Publishing.

Amrine, Frederick. 1998. "The Metamorphosis of the Scientist." In *Goethe's Way of Science*, edited David Seamon and Arthur Zajonc, 33–54 Albany: SUNY Press.

Amrine, Frederick R., and Francis J. Zucker. 1987. "Goethe and the Sciences." In *Goethe and the Sciences: A Reappraisal*, edited by Frederick R. Amrine, Francis J. Zucker, and Harvey Wheeler. Dordrecht: D. Reidel.

Anderson, A. B. 1975. "Combined Effects of Interpersonal Attraction and Goal Path Clarity on the Cohesiveness of Task-Oriented Groups." *Journal of Personality and Social Psychology* 31:68–75.

Barab, S., M. Gresalfi, and A. Ingram-Goble. 2010. "Transformational Play: Using Games to Position Person, Content, and Context." *Educational Researcher* 39 (7): 525–36.

Barab, S. and J. Plucker. 2002. "Smart People or Smart Contexts? Cognition, Ability, and Talent Development in an Age of Situated Approaches to Knowing and Learning." *Educational Psychologist* 37 (3): 165–82.

Barnes, H. 1980. "An Introduction to Waldorf Education." *Teachers College Record* 81 (3): 323–36.

Bartlett, F. C. 1932. *Remembering: A Study in Experimental and Social Psychology*. London: Cambridge University Press.

Baudrillard, Jean. 1995. *Simulacra and Simulation*. Ann Arbor: University of Michigan Press.

Benjamin, Walter. 1968. "On the Concept of History." In *Illuminations*, edited by Hannah Arendt, translated by Harry Zohn. New York: Harcourt, Brace and World.

Bhabha, Homi K. 1994. *The Location of Culture*. London: Routledge.

Billig, Michael, and Henri Tajfel. 1973. "Social Categorization and Similarity in Intergroup Behavior." *European Journal of Social Psychology* 3:27–52.

Bohannan, Laura. 1966. "Shakespeare in the Bush." *Natural History*, August–September.

Brown, Rupert. 2000. *Group Processes*.2nd ed. Kent: Blackwell.

Bruner, Jerome. 1991. "The Narrative Construction of Reality." *Critical Inquiry* 18 (1): 1–21.

———. 1993. "Do We 'Acquire' Culture or Vice Versa?" *Behavioral and Brain Science* 16 (3): 515–16.

———. 2002. *Making Stories: Law, Literature, Life*. New York: Farrar, Straus, Giroux.

———. 2004. "Life as Narrative." *Social Research* 71 (3): 691–710.

Cole, Michael. 1995a. "Socio-Cultural-Historical Psychology: Some General Remarks and a Proposal for a New Kind of Cultural-Genetic Methodology." In *Sociocultural Studies of Mind*, edited by J. Wertsch, P. Del Rio, and A. Alvarez, 187–214. New York: Cambridge University Press.

———. 1995b. "Cultural-Historical Psychology: A Meso-Genetic Approach." In *Sociocultural Psychology: Theory and Practice of Doing and Knowing*, edited by L. Martin, K. Nelson and E. Tobach, 168–204. Cambridge: Cambridge University Press.

———. 1996. *Cultural Psychology*. Cambridge, MA: Harvard University Press.

Cole, Michael, and the Distributed Literacy Consortium. 2006. *The Fifth Dimension: An After-School Program Built on Diversity*. New York: Russell Sage.

Cole, M., and P. Griffin. 1987. *Contextual Factors in Education: Improving Science and Mathematics Education for Minorities and Women*. Wisconsin Center for Education Research, School of Education, University of Wisconsin–Madison.

Cole, Michael, Karl Levitin, and Alexander Luria. 2006. *The Autobiography of Alexander Luria*. London: Erlbaum.

Darley, J., and C. D. Batson. 1973. "From Jerusalem to Jericho: A Study of Situational and Dispositional Variables in Helping Behaviour." *Journal of Personality and Social Psychology* 27:100–108.

Deutsch, Morton. 1949. "A Theory of Co-operation and Competition." *Human Relations* 2:129.

Dollard, Miller, et al. 1939. *Frustration and Aggression*. New Haven, CT: Yale University Press.

Downing-Wilson, Deborah. 2008. "Revealing Shifts in Attitude among Undergraduates Participating in Academic Service Learning Programs." *Operant Subjectivity: Journal of the International Society for the Scientific Study of Subjectivity* 30 (1): 1–2, 23–51.

Festinger, Leon. 1954. "A Theory of Social Comparison Processes." *Human Relations* 7:117–40.

Fine, Gary Alan. 1979. "Small Groups and Culture Creation: The Idioculture of Little League Baseball Teams." *American Sociological Review* 44 (5): 733–45.

———. 1987. *With the Boys: Little League Baseball and Preadolescent Culture*. Chicago: University of Chicago Press.

Geertz, Clifford. 1973. "Thick Description: Toward an Interpretive Theory of Culture." In *The Interpretation of Cultures: Selected Essays*, 3–30. New York: Basic Books.

Gergen, K. J., and M. M. Gergen. 1986. "Narrative Form and Construction of Psychological Science." In *Narrative Psychology: The Storied Nature of Human Conduct*, edited by T. Sarbin, 22–44. New York: Praeger.

———. 1997. "Narratives of the Self." In *Memory, Identity, Community: The Idea of Narrative in the Human Sciences*, edited by L. P. Hinchman and S. K. Hinchman, 161–84. Albany: SUNY Press.

Goethe, Johan Wolfgang. 1988a. *Faust*, pt. I. translated by P. Wayne. London: Penguin.

———. 1988b. "Empirical Observation and Science (Jan 15, 1798)." In *Goethe: Scientific Studies*, edited and translated by Douglas Miller. Boston: Suhrkamp.

Gresky, D., L. Ten Eyck, C. Lord, and R. McIntyre. 2005. "Effects of Salient Multiple Identities on Women's Performance under Mathematics Stereotype Threat." *Sex Roles* 53 (9/10): 703–16.

Hogg, M. A. 1992. *The Social Psychology of Group Cohesiveness: From Attraction to Social Identity*. London: Harvester Wheatsheaf.

Hutchins, Ed. 1996. *Cognition in the Wild*. Cambridge, MA: Bradford Books.

Johnson, D. W., G. Maruyama, R. Johnson, D. Nelson, and L. Skon. 1981. "Effects of Cooperative, Competitive, and Individualistic Goal Structures on Achievement: A Meta-analysis." *Psychological Bulletin* 89:47–62.

Kitchens, Marshall. 2002. *Ethnographic Identities: The Student Writer as Ethnographer*. Thomas R. Watson Conference on Rhetoric and Composition. Louisville, KY.

Kruglanski, A., J. Shah, A. Pierro, and L. Mannetti. 2002. "When Similarity Breeds Content: Need for Closure and the Allure of Homogeneous and Self-Resembling Groups." *Journal of Personality and Social Psychology* 83 (3): 648–62.

Kruglanski, Arie W., and Donna M. Webster. 1996. "Motivated Closing of the Mind: 'Seizing' and 'Freezing.'" *Psychological Review* 103 (2): 263–83.

Latane, Bibb. 1996. "Dynamic Social Impact: The Creation of Culture by Communication." *Journal of Communication* 46:13–25.

Latour, Bruno. 1996. "On Interobjectivity." *Mind, Culture, and Activity* 3 (4): 228–45.

Lemke, Jay. 2013. "Feeling and Meaning in the Social Ecology of Learning: Lessons from Play and Games." In *Affective Learning Together: Social and Emotional Dimensions in Collaborative Learning*, edited by Michael Baker, Jerry Anderson and Sanna Jarvella, 71–94. New York: Routledge.

Lewin, Kurt. 1948. *Resolving Social Conflicts*. Chicago: Harper and Row.

Luria, Alexander. 1928. The Problem of the Cultural Development of the Child. *Journal of Genetic Psychology* 35:493–506.

Mantovani, Guiseppe. 2000. *Exploring Borders: Understanding Culture and Psychology*. London: Routledge.

Morson, Gary. 1994. *Narrative and Freedom: The Shadows of Time*. New Haven: Yale University Press.

Nesbit, Edith. 1907. "Hamlet." In *Beautiful Stories by Shakespeare*. Toronto: Hertel.

Ochs, Elinor. 2011. "Narrative in Everyday Life." In *Discourse Studies: A Multidisciplinary Introduction*, edited by Teun A. van Dijk, 64–84. London: Sage.

Ochs, Elinor, and Lisa Capps. 2001. *Living Narrative: Creating Lives in Everyday Storytelling*. Cambridge, MA: Harvard University Press.

Paley, Vivian. 1986. *Boys and Girls: Superheroes in the Doll Corner*. Chicago: University of Chicago Press.

Palmer, Parker J., and Arthur Zajonc. 2010. *The Heart of Higher Education: A Call to Renewal*. San Francisco: Jossey-Bass.

Peckham, Morse. 1965. "In Man's Rage for Chaos." Chap. 2 in *The Dramatic Metaphor*. Philadelphia: Chilton Books.

Petrash, Jack. 2002. *Understanding Waldorf Education: Teaching from the Inside Out*. Beltsville, MD: Gryphon House.

Piaget, J. 1952. *The Origins of Intelligence in Children*. New York: International Universities Press.

Plotkin, H. 2003. *The Imagined World Made Real: Towards a Natural Science of Culture*. New Brunswick, NJ: Rutgers University Press.

Ricoeur, Paul. 1991. "Narrative Identity." In *On Paul Ricoeur: Narrative and Interpretation*, edited by D. Wood, 188–200. London: Routledge.

Rose, Edward, and William Felton. 1955. "Experimental Histories of Culture." *American Sociological Review* 20 (4): 383–92.

Rosenbaum, M. E., D. L. Moore, J. L. Cotton, M. S. Cook, R. A. Hieser, M. N. Shovar, and M. J. Gray. 1980. "Group Productivity and Process: Pure and Mixed Reward Structure and Task Interdependence." *Journal of Personality and Social Psychology* 39 (4): 626–42.

Rumelhart, D. E., P. Smolensky, J. L. McClelland, and G. E. Hinton. 1986. "Parallel Distributed Models of Schemata and Sequential Thought Processes." In *Parallel Distributed Processing: Explorations in the Microstructure of Cognition*, edited by J. L. McClelland and D. E. Rumelhart. Cambridge, MA: Bradford Books.

Sherif, Muzafer. 1966. *In Common Predicament: Social Psychology of Intergroup Conflict and Cooperation*. Boston: Houghton Mifflin.

Sherif, M., O. Harvey, B. White, W. Hood, and C. Sherif. (1954) 1988. *Intergroup Conflict and Cooperation: The Robbers Cave Experiment*. Middletown, CT: Wesleyan University Press.

Shih, M., T. L. Pittinsky, and N. Ambady. 1999. "Stereotype Susceptibility: Identity Salience and Shifts in Quantitative Performance." *Psychological Science* 10: 80–83.

Shirts, Garry. 1977. *BaFa BaFa: A Cross-Cultural Simulation*. Simulation Training Systems, Del Mar.

Steiner, Rudolf. 1968. *A Theory of Knowledge Implicit Based on Goethe's World Conception*. Translated by Olin Wannamaker. New York: Anthroposophic Press.

———. 2000. *Nature's Open Secret: Introductions to Goethe's Scientific Writings*. Hudson, NY: Anthroposophic Press.

Sullivan, Sherry, and Edward Duplaga. 1997. "The BaFa BaFa Simulation: Faculty

Experiences and Student Reactions." *Journal of Management Education* 21 (2): 265–72.

Tajfel, Henri. 1982. "Social Psychology of Intergroup Relations." *Annual Review of Psychology* 33:1–39.

Tajfel, H., M. Billig, R. Bundy, and C. Flament. 1971. "Social Categorization and Intergroup Behaviour." *European Journal of Social Psychology* 1:149–77.

Tajfel, Henri, and J. C. Turner. 1978. *Differentiation between Social Groups: Studies in the Social Psychology of Intergroup Relations.* European Association of Experimental Social Psychology. London: Academic Press.

Tomasello, M. 1999. *The Cultural Origins of Human Cognition.* Cambridge, MA: Harvard University Press

Vygotsky, Lev S. 1978. *Mind in Society: Development of Higher Psychological Processes.* Edited by M. Cole, V. John-Steiner, S. Scribner, and E. Souberman. Cambridge, MA: Harvard University Press.

———. 1994. *Thought and Language.* Edited by Alex Kouzlin. Cambridge, MA: MIT Press.

———. 2004. "Imagination and Creativity in Childhood." *Journal of Russian and East European Psychology* 42 (1): 7–97.

Watkins, John W. N. 1964. "Confession Is Good for Ideas." In *Intelligent Reading,* edited by B. M. W. Young and P. D. R. Gardiner. London: Longmans.

Wertsch, James. 1994. "The Primacy of Mediated Action in Sociocultural Studies." *Mind, Culture, and Activity* 1 (4): 202–8.

———. 1998. "Narrative as a Cultural Tool for Representing the Past." In *Mind as Action,* 73–108. New York: Oxford University Press.

———. 2001. "Sociocultural Approaches to Cognitive Development: The Constitutions of Culture in Mind." Introduction to special issue, *Human Development* 44 (2–3): 77–83. Edited by G. Hatano and J. V. Wertsch.

———. 2002. *Voices of Collective Remembering.* Cambridge: Cambridge University Press.

———. 2007. "National Narratives and the Conservative Nature of Collective Memory." *Neohelicon* 34 (2): 23–33.

Zajonc, Arthur. 1998. "Goethean Studies as a Science of the Future." In *Goethe's Way of Science: A Phenomenology of Nature,* edited by David Seamon and Arthur Zajonc, 299–314. Albany: SUNY Press.

INDEX

academic stereotype threat, 41

accommodation, 141–42

Alice and the unicorn (characters), 136

Alpha culture, 4, 11–12. *See also* Stone Soup group

Álvar Núñez Cabeza de Vaca, 126–27

Ambady, N., 41

Anderson, Alfred, 38–39, 86

angel of progress, the, 122, 159n10

artifacts, 73–76, 86–87, 139–42, 150

Asian students, 92–95, 100–103, 138–39

assimilation, 141–42

BaFa' BaFa' cultural simulation game, 3–5, 14, 22, 86, 141

Barab, S., 106

Bartlett, Frederic, 13–14, 106

Batson, Dan, 41

Baudrillard, Jean, 149–50

"Beat It," 34–35

Benjamin, Walter, 159n10

Beta culture, 4, 11–12. *See also* Fair Trade Cartel

Bhabha, Homi, 9

Bohannan, Laura, 143–44

Boys and Girls: Superheroes in Doll Corner (Paley), 75

Bruner, Jerome, 5–10, 87, 134

Capps, Lisa, 8, 9

cheating, 53–55

coconstitutive relationship between people and culture, 1–2, 5–6; context created by, 106–7; meaning-making and, 153–54. *See also* genesis of small-group culture; romantic science

Cody-Pfister, Rachel, 10–11

cognitive closure, 39–40

cohesion, 29–30, 38–39, 158n4, 158n6

Cole, Michael, 10, 106, 152

collective narrative process, x, 5–11, 134–38; embeddedness of narratives and, 143–44; multidimensional schemas constructed in, 13–14; student field notes in, 5, 10–11. *See also* narrative theories of culture

competition, ix–x

confessional style, x

context, 106–7

Darley, John, 41

demographics of the class, 11

Deutsch, Morton, 37–38

emotional dimensions of meaning-making, 153–54